Characters

To Tara Petersen,
Enjoy!
July 22nd 2020.

Other Books
By the Author:

Exposed to Winds

Construction Delay Claims

Anecdotes of Would-be Experts

Thoughts in a Maze

Trials & Errors, Laughs & Terrors

Characters

by

Arthur O.R. Thormann

Specfab Industries Ltd.

Edmonton, Alberta

2009

Library and Archives Canada Cataloguing in Publication

Thormann, Arthur O. R. (Arthur Otto Rudolf), 1934-
        Characters / by Arthur O.R. Thormann.

Short stories.
ISBN 978-0-9685198-6-8

        I. Title.

PS8589.H54945C44 2009   C813'.54   C2009-900240-X

Publisher: Specfab Industries Ltd.
                  13559 - 123A Avenue
                  Edmonton, Alberta, Canada
                  T5L 2Z1
                  Telephone: 780-454-6396

2nd Printing: PageMaster Publication Services Inc.
                  10180 - 105 Street
                  Edmonton, Alberta, Canada
                  T5J 1C9
                  Telephone: 780-425-9303

Cover Design: Carving replica of The Four Wise Monkeys: Speak
                  no evil, hear no evil, see no evil, and think no evil.

The stories in this book are based on the author's real life experiences
with the named characters.

These stories are a tribute to those
Who were part of them!

My gratitude goes to my daughter Nancy and my
friend Diana McLeod for their valued corrections of
my typos and faulty construction.

As always, all mistakes that remain are mine.

Preface

♣

Our own characters and lives are influenced and shaped by the characters we meet and with whom we associate. This is true whether or not the traits of the characters we meet are good. Think about it. Bad traits of other characters may well have shaped our characters in the opposite direction. Therefore, we owe a gratitude to all characters that have influenced our lives.

In this book, I picked ten characters that have centrally inspired my life. I could have easily picked many more characters of influence in my life, but the ten characters that I have chosen were the ones who were most influential in my life. Nevertheless, I will briefly mention a few characters in this preface that I have omitted.

Fritz Bruno Thormann, my father, and I have had a relatively brief relationship, but, for me, a very memorable one. In my second year of school, I came down with the whooping cough, and the school quarantined me. My father insisted that I should not lose a school year, so he decided to give me private lessons. Every day after we finished our supper, he spent three hours drilling me in the various school subjects. Then, he gave me a load of homework to do for the next day, until he came home to continue his drillings. When finally I returned to school, my teachers gave me some tests, and then reinstated me without any time lost. Soon after that, my father was drafted into the German army, and I only saw him on two more occasions, during his leaves. He died prematurely at age sixty-one.

Henry Butti was like a father to me. In 1934, the year when I was born, he co-founded the Progress Electric and Refrigeration Company. After Henry's partner died, he sold the company to Victor Webb, who renamed it, "Progress Electric Ltd." and stopped servicing refrigeration equipment. Henry started another company in the 1940s called Modern Electric.

In August 1953, I began my apprenticeship as an electrician with Progress Electric. When I completed my apprenticeship, Vic Webb promoted me to become his assistant manager and, eventually, his manager. After Henry sold his interest in Modern Electric and retired, I engaged him occasionally as a good-will ambassador on Progress Electric's projects. During this period, I really got to know Henry and his special qualities. Having spent many years in the field himself, Henry could empathize with the workers, and, at the same time, he also knew what was required in a business. Thus, Henry was able to give both me and our field workers good advice. Eventually, Henry and I developed a close and lasting friendship.

Henry was always a realistic critic. Whenever he felt strongly about some issue, he would not hesitate to write a letter to The Edmonton Journal, or to some offending authority, to make his views known in no uncertain terms. To my knowledge, the editor of The Edmonton Journal never refused to publish Henry's letters. Henry's perception and streetwise approach to issues always seemed to be welcome. I learned much from his criticisms.

However, what I'm most grateful for to Henry is that he taught me a deeper appreciation of operas. I went to see these stage shows before I knew Henry, to be sure, but I had no real grasp of them until Henry introduced me to some finer points behind the dramas and the music.

Walter Lawrence was the second president of the Electrical Contractors Association of Alberta. During his term, I was the president of the Edmonton Chapter and, thus, a director of the Association. Walter wasted no time to appoint me chairman of the Business and Public Relations Committee. He handed me a thick envelope full of instructions. The instructions covered everything from chairing meetings to various tasks that he wanted the committee to take on and complete during his presidency. I was ready and willing to accommodate him, and reported our progress at every directors' meeting.

I must say that I was very impressed with Walter's organizational ability, and I adopted some of his methods. Walter was also a critic, but in a helpful way. Whenever my committee was stuck on a task, Walter would offer some useful ways to proceed. Eventually, Walter and I became fast friends.

One of my committee's tasks was to convince our government to grant professional status for electrical contractors. We made an application to the government and received a favorable hearing. Then, Walter suddenly had second thoughts. As a professional electrical engineer himself, he had serious doubts about the electrical contractors' ability to handle professional status. I had a different opinion and continued my efforts to convince the government. Ultimately, our committee was successful, and Walter was very annoyed with me.

Don McKay was the secretary of the Edmonton Electrical Contractors Association when I was its president. He was extremely helpful to me. I also learned a thing or two from him about keeping proper minutes. When I reached the end of my term, he wrote a speech for me that I was to deliver at the President's Ball in the MacDonald Hotel. I read the speech several times and still couldn't get my mind around it. Uneasy, I finally went to Don and asked him if he minded if I wrote my own speech. He said he didn't mind, of course, but I could see that he was a little disappointed. Nevertheless, we stayed friends over the years. He phoned me many times for information on the various events in the association. After he retired, I met him occasionally at West Edmonton Mall, taking a walk. The last time I saw him, he proudly told me, "I'm eighty years old, you know." However, he only lived a short time after that and after his wife passed away.

Gerry Woods was a salesman of electrical materials. He worked for Northern Electric. As a salesman, Gerry never impressed me much. He was always crying the blues when I didn't favor him with orders. However, Gerry was a great fly fisherman. I'm still glad that he taught me the skill. Fishing the deep holes of the Wildhay River, I can still hear him say, "Your forearm must be an extension of the rod, Art. Never use your wrist. Let your elbow and your shoulder do the work!"

After a day or two of his instructions, I could usually land a fly within five feet of my target. Of course, he easily out-fished me. I was always amazed to watch him make a fly dance over the ripples of the river; some trout jumped visibly out of the water to catch it. Gerry was considerably overweight, and I was very sad when he died prematurely of a heart attack.

Gordon Michie was an electrical engineer. He worked for Progress Electric Ltd. as an estimator when I served my apprenticeship there. He taught me how to estimate electrical work, and we spent many an evening together discussing solutions to complex mathematical problems. We soon became firm friends. He even invited me to his home for Christmas dinner. His wife, Kay, usually spent all day roasting a big turkey. Gordon did the carving. When Kay saw me looking longingly at the carved-up bird, she laughed and said, "Gordon usually gets the parson's nose, but," she looked at Gordon with a hint in her eyes, "since you are our guest, I'm sure he'll offer it to you." Embarrassed, I asked her what she meant by the parson's nose. She laughed again and explained, "That juicy tail end you've been eyeing." Red in the face, I accepted it from Gordon, who smiled regretfully.

James Allan (Bud) Cameron and I were active on some Alberta Construction Association committees even prior to 1978, when we formed a partnership company to do some joint-venture work with a Saudi Arabian company. Three Alberta companies sponsored the partnership company: Fuller & Knowles Inc., represented by Jake Thygesen, J.K. Campbell & Associates Limited, represented by Bud Cameron, and

Progress Electric Ltd., represented by me. The plan had the support of the Alberta government. In September 1978, Bud, Jake and I had a few meetings in Edmonton to plan a trip to Saudi Arabia and discuss a few details regarding our approach with the Saudis.

In October, we left Edmonton at different times, but we agreed to meet in London, England, and, from there, take a Saudi airline to Jeddah.

In Jeddah, we met up with two Alberta government representatives, who had made the arrangements to meet with a sheikh and his manager to discuss a potential joint venture. We had two meetings with the sheikh and two meetings with his manager. At our second meeting with the sheikh, he seemed more interested in watching his imported video tapes than spending any more time with us.

However, we made good use of our time in Jeddah. We explored the city and took many construction-site pictures. We also spent an interesting evening with the sheikh's manager over dinner.

Before our final day in Jeddah, Jake had to leave, and Bud and I spent the last day visiting various construction sites and talking to construction managers and engineers. After we had had our supper on that last day, Bud and I summed up our findings in Jeddah. We agreed that doing business in Saudi Arabia may be riskier than we had anticipated. Inflation was rampant in the country, and the productivity of imported labor was down to a twenty-five percent level. Furthermore, a Saudi partnership appeared to be one-sided: Profits would be equally shared, but losses would belong to the off-shore partners.

Instead of heading back to Alberta immediately, I decided to stop in Frankfurt and visit some suppliers. I wanted to assure myself that the supply lines were in place in case we proceeded with the joint-venture.

This trip to Saudi Arabia and my time together with Bud brought me much closer to him, and I appreciated the insights he showed with respect to the underlying risks of doing business in a foreign country. He was a few years older than I, and I always respected his wisdom.

Dr. Robert MacGill took over from Dr. M.T. Richards, our first family doctor, when Dr. Richards moved to Vancouver, BC. I immediately liked Dr. MacGill and considered him to be as much of a friend as a doctor to me. Of course, I paid him visits only when necessary, but I always looked forward to these visits. We usually spent a few minutes talking of some private things. He told me, for example, that his mother believed in herbal remedies. He liked red wine, and he liked vacationing in Oregon. Dr. MacGill usually squeezed me in on the same day I phoned him for an appointment. He knew that I wouldn't ask for an appointment unless I had a serious ailment. When he retired, I should have been glad for him, but I was also sad to lose such a personable, understanding doctor.

And so on. I could expand the list of characters for a long time, with more names such as Sigrid Glimski, Edna Li, and Garth Myers. I could also include some early boyhood friends in a few more chapters, such as Klaus Frese, Helmut Hoffmann, and Manfred Betka, who were part of a salvage gang that extracted copper, zinc, lead, cast iron, and wood from the ruins of Berlin, and used the cash received for these treasures on the black market to obtain essential food and supplies for their families. Furthermore, I could also have written some chapters about the chaps with whom I apprenticed at Zeiss Ikon, such as Klaus Groth, Guenther Warmbier, and Lutz Brachold, and I could have added friends like Peter Roeckenwagner, to whom I owed my first inklings of electronics.

As it is, I limited myself to the ten following character chapters, starting with my mother, who was a major influence in my life. Additionally, I added an appendix with a list of strange assertions by some well-known characters. I have also included my comments on them. These assertions have provided me with food for thought, and I hope that they will also provide you with similar stimulations.

One last comment: Regarding The Four Wise Monkeys on the front cover, some folks believe that the fourth monkey depicts *do no evil*; it actually depicts *think no evil*.

Arthur O.R. Thormann
January 2009

Contents

Angelika Jeske

Angelika was a perpetual fountain of wisdom. She was also what is commonly known as streetwise. She was a witty and entertaining woman, who saw some humor in every situation and a silver lining in every dark cloud. Whenever one of her humorous, witty remarks offended someone, she would laugh and quickly declare, "I'll take it all back and assert the opposite!"

Angelika was born in a small German colony near Novograd Wolynsk in the Ukraine. Before she was two years old, her parents immigrated to Germany with her and her half-brother. In her Ukrainian birth certificate, she was named Agathe,[1] the German version of Agatha, but all her life she was only known by the names of Angelita or Angelika.[2] I shall henceforth refer to her as Angelika, the official name she used during her life in Canada.

Angelika has had a relatively hard life in Germany, and, come to think of it, in Canada as well. Nevertheless, it never seemed to dampen her spirits except, perhaps, during the last year of her life, when her sickness sapped some energy out of her. Her parents were poor, and they placed much demand on their children after WWI, during the inflationary 1920s in Germany. In 1930, her father decided to leave

---

[1] The last syllable of this name is pronounced "teh" as in Tehran.
[2] This name is pronounced Angeleeka as opposed to Angelica.

Germany and reestablish himself in Canada, but he only scraped enough money together for his and his youngest son's fares. Angelika had to fend for herself until she married Fritz Thormann in 1933.

Angelika: She was elegant, composed, and beautiful.

My conscious focus on Angelika's qualities started in 1942. After the German army drafted my father, Angelika assumed the role of sole leadership, and she lived up to it admirably. We lived in Berlin, and Berlin seemed to be the focal point of WWII at the time. I still remember the sirens going off at night to alert us to an imminent air attack, which meant getting up quickly and running down from the fourth floor to the basement for shelter. Sometimes Angelika would stop on the main floor for a peek outside. Usually, all we saw were crisscrossing light beams in the dark sky that tried to identify aircraft, and all we heard were antiaircraft flaks. However, when Angelika heard bombs dropping nearby, she would quickly rush us down into the basement shelter. In the shelter, most of the apartment dwellers looked tired and scared, but, for my sisters and me, the true reality and seriousness of war had not yet registered. We still viewed these events with a childish excitement. We also had fun during the morning after the air attacks gathering shrapnel, which we used to trade with each other, until the government decided to collect the shrapnel to build more bombs.

Angelika and her women friends were undeterred by the wartime conditions and found plenty of time to get together and enjoy themselves. Berlin seemed to be the transit station for many soldiers on the way to the front lines. They, too, were unnaturally joyful – almost too joyful in light of the terrible bombings every day. I still remember one jolly soldier by the name of Joseph Rommel, who said that there was nothing to worry about and assured the women that the war wouldn't last much longer. His easy-going, carefree nature charmed Angelika, who had befriended him, but he was soon moved to the Russian Front, and we never heard from him again.

In August of 1943, Angelika gave birth to a third daughter. By then, bombings had become critical in Berlin, and women and children were evacuated. The government sent me temporarily to foster parents near Poznan, and as soon as Angelika had recovered sufficiently to travel, the government sent her and my sisters to a farmyard near Finsterwalde. I joined them there a few months later.

As a rule, Angelika made friends easily, both male and female, but she had problems with the farmer, a gruff, old man, who hated urbanites. Eventually, we moved to a house owned by a couple in a small village called Groebitz, who reluctantly made their second floor available to us. The owners provided these facilities on government orders instead of renting them. Angelika's half-brother's wife, Anni, and her two children joined us there as well, and since the second floor consisted of barely 800 square feet, the two women with their six children were very crowded, but they coexisted in good spirits until the end of the war.

In April 1945, when some retreating German soldiers came through Groebitz, Angelika and Anni met a homeopathic practitioner who gave them a herbal powder made from an African plant that was supposed to trigger abortions. He said it might be useful if the advancing Russians raped them. However, neither Angelika nor Anni had to use it. When the Russians did arrive in Groebitz, Angelika and Anni befriended a German-speaking Russian officer who provided them with badly needed food, and, under his envisaged protection, other Russian soldiers did not dare to bother the two women – they were even friendly and helpful.

Nevertheless, soon after the war ended in Germany, Angelika became restless. She decided to head back to Berlin with her children, and the two women parted tearfully. Fearing worse conditions in Berlin, Anni had decided to stay in Groebitz for a while longer.

Berlin was plainly a disaster area in 1945. The apartment building where we had lived had also been destroyed, and accommodations in the city were at a premium and barely inhabitable. Fortunately, Angelika's Aunt Ottilie made her small apartment in the urban area available to Angelika and her children, because she and her daughter, Edith, had taken up "safer" residence in their garden-colony cabin, which also gave them more immediate access to their garden products and the rabbits they raised out there. As it turned out, the garden-colony cabin was not so safe, after all – barely a year later, Aunt Ottilie, Edith, and Edith's fiancé were murdered in it.

Accommodations were one thing, and potable water, adequate food, and heating fuel were another. The city's water supply system was inoperative, and the river and canal were badly contaminated. Fortunately, the city had quite a number of water hand pumps, but the wait time in lineups was fairly long, just to fill a couple of pails. Under these conditions, typhoid fever and cholera were widespread in the city.

Food was rationed, and Angelika had quite a time managing these rations. Rations were based on the daily need for calories – physical workers were rated at the highest level, of course, and all others got barely enough to survive. Whenever Angelika failed to manage the rations, we went hungry for a few days, unless the grocer took pity on us and advanced us some food on future rations – which meant, of course, that Angelika had to start managing more strictly. However, she was also a resourceful woman. She would liberally use items that were not rationed, like cod-liver oil, castor oil,[3] sorrel, and such. Most of these items didn't appeal to our taste buds but were very effective to keep us alive and healthy.

Heating fuel, consisting mainly of coal and wood, was made available only to life-supporting industries, such as bakeries. The population at large had to beg, borrow, or steal their fuel to keep warm during the winter. After scrounging the remaining wood from the ruins around them, most folks burned their furniture next. The weakest of the elderly people just died.

All these shortages created a thriving black market, but a person had to have the required money or other means to trade in it. Fortunately, the scrap-metal business was also flourishing. This enabled people to gather from the ruins lead pipes, copper pipes, and cast-iron radiators, and sell these to scrap dealers for some extra money to buy other necessities on the black market. Additionally, those who were fortunate enough to get the occasional parcel from relatives in the USA or Canada usually traded their acquired cigarettes and coffee for more useful or edible products. All the same, for most people supplies remained short.

On the other hand, divorces, as another casualty of war, were on the increase. Angelika and Fritz were no exception. Fritz never did return to Berlin, he found another woman in Schleswig Holstein, and Angelika's

---

[3] Castor oil loses its effect after it is heated up over 80°C.

lawyer and friend, Willi Kuenzel, took care of the legal formalities of the divorce. Willi Kuenzel was quite a humorist. He described the world, mainly himself, in funny poems, where he used the nickname Kuelli Winzel. Eventually, Angelika came across a chap called Hans Hammel. Hans had been a paratrooper during the war. He was good looking, tall, and blond, but slightly balding, and he didn't mind marrying a woman with four children, who was getting parcels from Canada. But the marriage didn't last long. Besides being good looking, Hans turned out to be gay. One day, he came home with gonorrhea, and that ended the marriage as far as Angelika was concerned.

During the depression of the 1930s, Angelika's father, Reinhold, and his youngest son, Rudolph, worked a homestead in Alberta, Canada. After three years of hard work, in 1933, they had saved enough money to bring over Reinhold's second son, Albert. It took another two years for Reinhold to bring his wife, Henriette, to Canada. Angelika was next in line, but Reinhold couldn't scrape enough money together to bring her, her husband and her children to Canada before WWII broke out. In addition, after WWII, immigration laws were stiffer. It took six more years to satisfy the authorities and make the necessary arrangements to bring Angelika and her four children to Canada, the land where milk and honey flows.

As it turned out, milk and honey did not flow for Angelika and her children for a while. To start with, living conditions on her father's farm were still primitive. Things got even worse after her half-brother,

Alex, and his family arrived on the farm from Germany. Then there were religious clashes. Angelika was a Baptist, her father was a Lutheran, her youngest brother belonged to the main group of the Pentecostal Church, and her mother and second brother belonged to a splinter group of the Pentecostal Church, which they had formed in Barrhead, Alberta. All were vying for Angelika's support, but, ignoring the gratitude she owed them, she refused to abandon her own religious beliefs in favor of one of theirs.

To get away from the conflict, Angelika took a farm job with a nearby Polish family, who were almost hostile towards her. While she worked there, she met a visiting chap by the name of John Skolimoski, who tried to talk her into coming to work at his place. He owned a sheep farm about twenty kilometers further north of Barrhead. She accepted his invitation on the condition that she could bring her three daughters along. After all, she reasoned, she had to look after her children, which she had been doing most of her adult life. He was only too happy to oblige her, and she eventually married him six years later. The marriage was more one of convenience than of passionate love. In any case, moving to John's farm did not improve Angelika's living conditions, which remained primitive for many years. He eventually did build a new house for her, including electric lights, a gas furnace, indoor toilet facilities, and running water, all of which were missing in his old shack of a house.

John tried his best to make Angelika happy. He took her to town for shopping whenever she felt like it.

♣

He bought her and her daughters everything they needed. He took her visiting to his friends. He entertained her friends and family members, whenever they came to his farm. He taught her how to drive his car. He built her a new house. And he tried to humor her when she appeared unhappy. Yet, a deep sadness lingered with Angelika. She was like a fish out of water. Although she had picked up the English language sufficiently to get by, she was never as fluent in it as she was in the German language. This may have been the reason why some of her Berliner wittiness had also disappeared.

Eventually, John turned bitter. He resentfully complained about his lot in life to his friends and anyone else who cared to listen to him. He felt nobody appreciated him enough. His health was failing him, too. He struggled for a while with various ailments and finally succumbed to pneumonia in November of 1974. Angelika remained on the farm for another nineteen years. During this time, she befriended a retired farmer named Manuel Bilau, who offered to help her manage John's farm, but it was soon apparent that with Manuel's help they mismanaged more than managed the farm. Angelika had rented the farm to another farmer on a percentage-crop-share basis, which yielded her around $3,600 per year. Come harvest time, Manuel and Angelika counted the truckloads of grain the renter removed, and Manuel concluded that the renter shortchanged her. Angelika was upset about this and asked me to help her find another renter.

This task was clearly not part of my expertise, and

I set out to inform myself properly. I bought a book on farm rentals and spent quite a bit of time getting familiar with the necessary farm-rental conditions – seeding and fertilizing requirements, summer fallow obligation, fence and building maintenance, and such. I even met with our lawyer, Carl Leviston, who was a landowner and had a good knowledge of farm-rental details. Next, I bought a farm-rental-agreement form and drove to Angelika's farm to make the necessary arrangements for a new renter.

I explained my preparations to Angelika, and she told me sheepishly that Manuel and she had already engaged another renter. I was dumbfounded.

"You mean I've done all this work for nothing?" I demanded to know.

"We hadn't heard anything from you for a while," she answered, "and we thought we should take advantage of the opportunity that came along to get a new renter." Manuel just sat there giving me his perpetual smirk. He had obviously exercised a lot of influence over Angelika.

"What kind of an agreement did you sign?" I wanted to know.

Angelika got up to get a shoebox, where she kept her papers. She took out a piece of paper with some scribbles on it and showed it to me. "I made notes of what we'd agreed on," she explained.

I couldn't believe my eyes. "There's nothing here about summer fallow or building and fence maintenance, or any other obligations of the renter," I said. "It just says he'll pay you $2,000 per year."

"He's a farmer," Manuel, contemptuously, piped up, "and he knows what needs to be done to a farm."

"I know he is a farmer, but does he know that he is obligated to do what needs to be done? Has he signed an agreement to that effect? And what about the rental term: When does it start and end?"

"It starts in spring, and it ends when Angelika wants it to end," said Manuel, smirking at me.

"We trust him," said Angelika, plaintively. "At least he won't cheat me. I won't have to count the truckloads of grain he removes, and I'll get a steady $2,000 every year."

"That figure tells me he's already cheating you," I said dejectedly. Manuel shook his head as if to say, you don't know what you're talking about. Angelika just shrugged her shoulders.

After Manuel died in 1993, Angelika put the farm up for sale. This must have upset her new renter, because he refused to pay her for the last year's rent. She issued a statement of claim against him, of course, but, in the end, she settled for a reduced amount of $1,500 rather than proceeding to trial against him.

While her farm was up for sale, Angelika moved to an apartment in Barrhead. She seemed to be happier there, at least not as lonely. Eventually, she met another retired farmer named Oscar Shier. They decided to share her apartment to keep the costs down. Angelika and Oscar had a few good years together. Both in their eighties, they supported each other well. Then, Angelika had a mild stroke, and when Oscar slipped in the bathtub and hurt his hip, she was powerless to help him get out. Oscar had to have an operation. The operation itself was successful, yet, he died a few days later. Soon afterward, Angelika ended up in the Barrhead hospital for various treatments. The hospital eventually transferred her to a nursing home. The staff at the nursing home looked after her well, but one day she had a bad fall and broke her hip. This seemed to rob her of her remaining energy. A few weeks after this mishap, Angelika died peacefully, on March 12th 2004.

The relatively primitive conditions during Angelika's first twenty years in Canada, and the unhappy family relationship that had met her when she arrived at her father's farm, were quite a culture shock for her – in her mind, even the postwar conditions of the bombed city of Berlin had been better. During those first years in Canada, she regretted many times leaving Germany. Nevertheless, setting personal considerations aside, Angelika's life was a definite success just looking after the interests of her children: first during the terrible times of WWII, then during the postwar years, and finally during her adverse circumstances in Canada. Angelika never wavered when it came to deciding between her welfare and the welfare of her children.

2

Herr Mueller

Herr Mueller was the master mechanic at Zeiss Ikon in Berlin, Germany, with whom I commenced my precision-instrument mechanic's apprenticeship on April 1ˢᵗ 1949. Four new apprentices started on that day.

Herr Mueller was a hard taskmaster – no pun intended. To get us started, he gave each of us a rusty, six-centimeter steel cube and told us to file it down to an exact dimension of five centimeters. He also gave us some instructions on how to go about the filing task, using first rough and then fine files. Then, he stressed the near-zero tolerances he expected in the finished product. Looking bored, none of us had the slightest idea of the hardships those expected tolerances would entail.

He assigned each of us an individual work area that included one vise and one tool drawer along a workbench. After the master gave us more instructions on how to use the vise without damaging the faces of the clamped product, each of us had to start smooth-filing one surface of the cube. The idea was to file it absolutely flat. This turned out to be quite a trick. Herr Mueller came around occasionally and put a straightedge to the surface in all directions, including the diagonal. He shook his head sadly. "You have a slight hump on the surface," he advised each of us in turn. "Instead, try to file a slight valley, and, hopefully, you may end up with a flat surface." Believe it or not, I was unable to file the surface flat enough to get the master's approval on that first day, and I started to get a very slight inkling of what lay ahead of me to file all six surfaces flat. When I say "a very slight inkling," what I mean is that I still didn't realize the hardships I would encounter to file adjacent surfaces exactly at ninety degrees to each other, and when I say "exactly," I mean at near-zero tolerance.

Our workdays started at 7:15 a.m. and ended at 5:00 p.m. Each day, five minutes before quitting time, we had to wrap up the products we were working on (in this case, the steel cubes) in clean rags, put them and our tools in our drawers, remove all filings and other unnecessary items from our work areas, and wipe them clean with linseed oil.

We all worked several weeks on our cubes. Two apprentices, after failing to file their cubes to meet Herr Mueller's exact tolerances, continued to file a few more weeks, trying to reach a new dimension. In their cases, Herr Mueller had destroyed their first attempt by flattening a corner of their cubes on a steel leveling plate on his desk. Both apprentices came out of his office with tears in their eyes. I, too, went tearfully home on many days and told my mother that, perhaps, I had chosen the wrong trade.

I recall that I was the first to finish my cube – to Herr Mueller's satisfaction, that is. I was elated, but, again, I'd had no inkling of my next agonies. The master gave me new instructions with respect to a groove he wanted me to file in each of three of my cube's surfaces: one rectangular groove, one triangular groove, and one round groove – in that order. Naturally, Herr Mueller's tolerances did not change. Before I left his office, he demonstrated his accuracy demands by showing me a cube finished by another apprentice some time back. He took a short, one-centimeter diameter, ground, round, steel rod out of his desk drawer, slid it into the round groove of the cube, turned the cube up-side down, and smiled as the rod stuck in the groove. (It was the first time I'd ever seen him smile.) Then, he looked at me gravely and said, "This is the accuracy I expect from you." I was appropriately awed, of course, thanked him, and left his office. I still do not know to this day why I thanked him, because the distress I had experienced trying to meet his expectations is beyond words.

After I finally finished my cube with the three grooves to Herr Mueller's satisfaction, stamped my employee number into one surface, and turned it over to him for safekeeping, I noticed a distinct change in attitude towards me by the master. His instructions for my training became much friendlier – almost as if I had passed a critical assessment in his eyes. Likewise, my attitude towards Herr Mueller changed. I had gained a new respect for what he was trying to accomplish, and, from then on, I became more self-disciplined, drawing less criticism from him.

It was already late afternoon, and he told me to clean my files and pack up. Cleaning the files was a regular chore. We used chalk, of course, to keep the accumulation of filings in the file's ridges to a minimum. Nevertheless, we had to clean the files fairly often, pushing a piece of tin brass along the file's ridges. Otherwise, the filings stuck in the ridges would cause unwanted etchings in the filed surfaces.

Next morning, I went into the master's office. He was busy with one of the journeymen who supervised some women in the mass production department. I waited patiently for them to finish their discussion. Then, the master told me to sit in the chair opposite his desk. He took a small drawing out of one of his desk drawers and put it in front of me. I recognized the shape of a hammer. It had all the required dimensions shown – even for the convex outline of the hole.

"I hope you didn't think you were finished with filing," said Herr Mueller. Did I detect a gloating look on his face?

"As a matter of fact, yes, I thought I was finished with filing," I replied.

"Well, your next project will add a few more facets to your training," he said. "In addition to accuracy, you must learn a few things about hardening and tempering steel. This requires a slight over-dimension when you're finished filing, a fraction of a millimeter, so that when the slag is polished off, after hardening, your final dimensions will end up accurate. Remember this: Your finished product must weigh exactly one-hundred grams. Now, go and do your filing and see me when you're finished. Then, I'll teach you how to harden and temper the steel. Take the drawing along."

Herr Mueller

♣

I had mixed feelings about this project. I was excited about the new facets, of course, but I was also apprehensive about the warning that the finished product must weigh exactly one-hundred grams. What if it didn't?

Even the filing task turned out to be more difficult than I had expected, especially for the convex-shaped hole. It took me several days to get all the various dimensions right. Herr Mueller came around a few times, watching my efforts, but I was unable to detect any sentiment in his expressionless demeanor. When I finished filing, I took the hammer into his office. He looked at it, nodded, and said, "Let's go down to the forge, and I'll teach you to harden steel." In the forge, he told me to fill the hole in the hammer with clay, to protect it during heating and the subsequent chilling in cold water. After I had filled the hole with clay, he heated the hammer to a red glow, explaining to me the right color he tried to obtain, and then dipped it quickly in a pail of cold water. It gave off a hissing sound, and the water boiled violently around the hammer; a cloud of steam rose quickly to the ceiling. When he removed the hammer, it looked as black as coal, and he said, "There'll be some slag on the surface. You'll have to polish it off with emery paper until you reach the final dimensions. Come and see me again when you're finished, and I'll show you how to temper it properly."

I found polishing the hammer harder than I had expected. I had to be very careful to maintain the flat surfaces and sharp edges. Furthermore, I had to attain my final dimensions, so that the hammer would weigh exactly one hundred grams. By the end of the day, I was sweating, but I felt certain the master would be pleased with the end product. I went to his office first thing in the morning. He looked at the hammer critically and then put it on his scale. "One hundred grams," he said. "Now let's go down and temper it." I breathed out a sigh of relief. As he lit the blowtorch, Herr Mueller explained to me that the hammer before tempering is as hard as glass and may shatter with a good knock. "The idea is," he said, "to keep the hammering edges hard but soften the center, where the hole is located. Now, pay attention." I watched him gently heat the center of the hammer until it turned a brownish yellow color. Amazingly, this color spread slowly to the hammering edges and the center turned to a grayish blue color. At this point, the master quickly dipped the hammer into a pail of cold water. The colors remained visible after chilling the hammer. Herr Mueller gave me one of his fleeting smiles. "That's how it's done," he said. "Remember the procedures for all future tools that require hardening and tempering."

"I have one final filing project for you," Herr Mueller continued. "I want you to file a little milling tool for countersinking screws. First, I'll show you how to turn out the basic shape of the borer on the lathe. Then, you must file twenty-four saw-toothed ridges to form the milling surface of the tool. Finally, the tool must be hardened and tempered, similar to what I have taught you to do with the hammer." Herr Mueller took a drawing from his desk and handed it to me. "These are your final dimensions," he concluded.

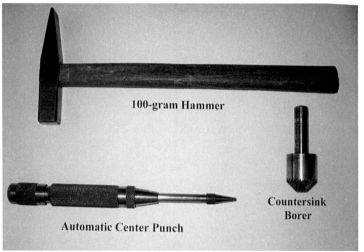

These are some of the more difficult tools I've had to make at Zeiss.

In a way, I was thrilled. Not only was I ahead of the other apprentices, but I was also the first to use a lathe. Next morning, after I picked up some stock from the storeroom, Herr Mueller patiently explained to me some of the basics regarding the use of the lathe. Then he watched me as I tried to turn out the countersink borer, frequently offering hints. We took most of the morning to turn out the basic form of the tool. In retrospect, the task seems to be fairly simple, but, at the time, I was perspiring.

I spent all afternoon inscribing the lines for the saw-toothed ridges on the milling surface of the tool. Nevertheless, the hard part came when I started to file these ridges. The round, cone-shaped surface made the filing task extremely difficult, since the milling edges had to conform to the shape turned out on the lathe.

Herr Mueller had explained at the outset that a failure to maintain the format of the milling edges would make the tool vibrate, and, thus, make a smooth surface of the countersunk hole unattainable.

After many hours of finicky work, I came to an end of my filing task and went to Herr Mueller for his approval. He took a critical look at the milling edges and nodded. I was relieved. Then he said, "The test comes after hardening and tempering. We'll see if your tool can produce a smooth surface."

He accompanied me to the forge building and watched me harden and temper the tool, with an occasional grunt of approval. Back upstairs, before I put the tool to the test, he explained to me the various lubricants I had to use, depending on the material I was cutting. We picked a steel plate, which required the standard cutting oil. I drilled a three-eighths inch hole and then used my tool to mill the countersunk surface. The tool didn't vibrate and the surface was smooth. Herr Mueller gave me one of his rare smiles. He said, "Come and see me in the morning for a more difficult project."

For some reason, perhaps because I was the first to finish my filing projects, Herr Mueller took more of an interest in my ongoing training. First, he introduced me to the drilling machine and showed me how to sharpen drills properly. Then, he showed me how to use the lathe and how to make my own cutting tools for use with the lathe. Next, I had to turn out a number of punching tools on the lathe, all of which entailed, again, hardening and tempering the steel. After a few weeks of lathe work, Herr Mueller introduced me to the milling machine. He started giving me tool projects for mass-production work. I learned how to use the pitch circle to cut gears, how to wind coil springs from piano wire, how to shape metal by hammering or by forming on the lathe, how to forge steel tools, and how to use ordinary, as well as silver, solder on brass products. Never a day went by when I wasn't extremely interested in my work. This also got Herr Mueller more fired up, and he was very pleased to show me all the tricks of the trade.

At the beginning of my second year, Herr Mueller gave me a special test project, to make an automatic center punch. He gave me a drawing and some basic instructions and told me to get started. A center punch is used to create an indentation, a small crater, as it were, in a piece of metal to help a drill bit get started at an exact location. Normally, to accomplish this task, we use a hand-held punch and a hammer. The automatic center punch eliminates the use of the hammer – it has a built-in, spring-loaded rod that acts as a hammer. When you push the body of the tool down, a hammering rod is released and pounds on another rod that holds the center punch. The diameter of the body of the tool is 15 mm, and the extended length of the tool measures 18 cm. It consists of eleven parts, including three internal springs. The top end of the tool consists of a screw cap that can compress a spring to adjust the strength of the pounding.

Literally, most of my training to that point went into the creation of this tool. It took me a few days to finish it, and I took it proudly to the master. He looked at it critically and tried it out on his leveling plate. Then, he adjusted the pounding strength, tried it again, and nodded his approval. "Very good," he said.

For my future work, Herr Mueller assigned me to a journeyman who manufactured tools for mass-production projects. This was the real thing, as far as I was concerned. I was now part of a process that actually created the final products for public use, mostly cameras, but also microscopes and other instruments. I enjoyed my second year immensely. Herr Mueller still kept a close watch on me, giving me the odd tip when he felt I needed it.

Towards the end of my second year, my mother wrote to Zeiss Ikon, explaining that we were immigrating to Canada and asking for my release. The managers of the company and especially Herr Mueller were very unhappy about this request, and, for a while, it looked like they may refuse it. However, maternal guidance prevailed, and the day came when I had to say good-bye to Herr Mueller. He allowed me to take along the tools I had made (except the cube I had filed) and wished me luck in the "Wild West." He expressed the hope that I could make use of my skills in Canada, a country only occupied by farmers, trappers, miners, Indians and Eskimos, we thought. Sadly, he shook his head and turned to other, pressing matters.

In my later years, I appreciated the training I had received from Herr Mueller more than I had let him know on that last day. Yes, he was a hard taskmaster, but he only had the best in mind for his apprentices.

3

Alphonse Pfiffner

During my first year in Canada, I stayed with Dr. Alphonse Pfiffner for about five months. He wasn't really a medical doctor – more accurately, a herbalist – but everyone called him doctor, or Old Doc. He told me that he had actually finished his medical doctor's curriculum in Switzerland, but, after he had failed the MD's examinations, he had decided to switch to herbal medicine. There was no doubt: he was extremely knowledgeable in the field of herbal remedies.

Dr. Pfiffner had a small house and about ten acres of land, where he grew all kinds of herbs, a little over a mile from my grandfather's farm. In July 1951, I had an accident on my grandfather's farm, jabbing a rotten root into the lower part of my right shin. My grandfather had pulled the broken-off root out of my shin and put some antiseptic solution on it, but even though the wound healed after a week, the shin still hurt. My grandfather took me into town to have X-rays made, but the X-rays did not show anything abnormal. However, I could hardly walk. When I heard about Dr. Pfiffner, I decided to hobble along the mile to his place to ask him if he could help me. He took one look at my shin and told me there was still an infection left and he would have to open the wound again to drain the puss.

I must have looked worried; he laughed and said, "Don't worry. I won't *cut* it open – I'm not allowed to

23

use the knife – I have herbal means to open wounds. But you should stay with me for a few days."

I assured him that this is not a problem as long as he lets my mother know where I am.

He proceeded immediately to boil some water. He added some powder to the boiling water, which, as I found out later, was ground comfrey root, and stirred it to a thick paste. Then he applied the paste to the wound and covered it with gauze, which he taped in place.

"That should do it, for now," he said. "I'll change it once a day."

After a few days, the wound had indeed opened up, and some puss began to drain from it. This development pleased the doctor. He waited two or three days until he saw a trickle of blood and then applied some Ozonol antiseptic cream to the open wound. "It's the best ointment I know of – marvelous," he assured me. "They use it in hospitals." A few days later, the wound had healed again, although a slight swelling remained. However, I walked again without pain.

Old Doc asked me to stay with him for a while and help him gather herbs. He promised to pay me a little and provide me with meals and lodging. I agreed. As we walked through the fields and forests, he pointed out various differences between herbs and their remedial qualities.

Sometimes he said, "People consider this plant to be a nuisance, a weed. They would be very surprised if I pointed out to them what tremendous healing power it possesses."

He also gave me books on herbs to read. I sat up many an evening until midnight to study these books.

I remember the day when someone, a relative, I think, delivered an elderly man to Old Doc. He couldn't walk anymore, and we carried him into Old Doc's living room. His medical doctors had told him there was nothing they could do for him. He told Old Doc that he was the president of the Northern Alberta Railroad and that money was no object, as long as Old Doc could restore him to health. Old Doc looked at him sadly and promised him that he would do everything humanly possible. He requested me to bring in a few pails full of water, which he brought to a boil on the stove, adding a few branches of juniper with berries still attached. Then, he and I dumped the boiling liquid into his bathtub. We added some cold water to bring the temperature down to a level just bearable. Next, we carried our guest into the bathroom and lowered him into the bathtub. Old Doc covered him with a woolen blanket so that only his head was still visible. The old man had to sweat it out for a good half hour. Then, we lifted him out of the bathtub and carried him back into the living room. We placed him on the sofa, which was going to be his bed for a few weeks. Old Doc prepared a tea for him to drink and then started to prepare supper. Supper, with some regularity in Old Doc's house, consisted of a potato and vegetable soup with chunks of ham sausage. "Very nourishing," Old Doc assured me.

We gave the old man a similar bath and cup of tea

each day for a fortnight. Gradually, the old man began to use his limbs again. After a fortnight, he started to walk around slowly, with the help of a cane. Old Doc told him we would continue to treat him for a few more days. "Then," he said, "I'll give you enough herbs to take home so that you can treat yourself." When the old man left us, he walked out of the house without a cane. He hugged Old Doc and almost cried he was so thankful.

This elderly man wasn't the only one I watched Old Doc heal. People came to him with stomach ulcers, diabetes, rheumatic, and arthritic problems, and even cancer. Old Doc had a remedy for each of them. His main staple was the comfrey root. He used it primarily for stomach and intestinal problems. He mixed the comfrey root with a bit of senna and some Bismarex and packaged this mixture in a small carton. He explained to me that the main ingredient, the comfrey root, had drawing qualities, drawing out the poisons or infections; the senna he added to induce bowel movements, to get rid of the bad products, and the Bismarex, a commercial product sold at that time by Rexall, he added because of its healing quality. He was so proud of the effectiveness of his mixture that he had even registered a patent for it.

Many of his patients wrote to him for help, and he sent his cures all over North America. He showed me many letters of thanks from people who were cured by him. However, he also had some disagreements with the American and Canadian Medical Associations. They considered him nothing more than a quack.

Nevertheless, he had a large following of cured patients who believed in him explicitly.

We spent many an evening together when he lectured me about the healing powers of various herbs. One evening, he had gone to bed early, and I was still sitting in the living room, reading one of his books on herbs. He must have had a sexual urge, because suddenly he came back out and showed me his half-erect penis. "Could you stroke it a bit for me?" he said, "I can't get it up any more." I had heard about his homosexual tendencies, and I flatly told him that I wasn't into that sort of thing. He just grunted and went back to his bedroom. After that rejection, he never bothered me again.

In September, we dug out his seasoned comfrey roots. He was very proud of his acre of comfrey. "I imported the plants from Siberia," he assured me. "They are the best." We washed the roots and surface-dried them in the sun for a while. Then, we dried them to bone-hardness in his attic. When he had enough of them dried, he ground them to powder with his hammer mill and stored the powder in dark jars, ready for further processing.

I used all my spare moments in the fall to split wood for him, which I piled up along the side of his house for use in his stove during the winter. Off and on, I also hired myself out to farmer friends of Old Doc, to help them bundle and stook their various grain crops. Many times, the awns of the barley chafed my arms and chest, and I had to apply some of Old Doc's "marvelous" ointment, Ozonol, to heal them.

♣

The farmers paid me one dollar per acre for stooking. On good days, I earned ten dollars. Old Doc was more generous. For a day's wood splitting, he paid me twenty dollars.

Winter came early in 1951. To keep myself busy, I helped Ted Morris, another friend of Old Doc, who ran a service garage in Barrhead. Mainly, he replaced motor parts of farm tractors. The work didn't even come close to my trade experience at Zeiss Ikon, but, at least, it was better than wood splitting and farming. Ted Morris eventually referred me to Jimmy Dawson, a friend of his in Edmonton, who ran a company called Edmonton Auto Parts. I started to work for Jimmy in January 1952. My first task consisted of turning out parts on the lathe – at last, I was one step closer to my precision-mechanic's trade.

Leave-taking from Old Doc was an almost teary affair. We had grown fond of each other. He offered me a drink of his favorite scotch whisky: White Horse. We drank to my future. I promised to pay him a visit as often as possible, which I did. However, in November 1954, I heard that he had died in a fire that burned down his house. The investigators assumed that a makeshift oil heater might have caused the fire. He probably wanted to save himself chopping some wood. I felt very sad. I will always remember my good times with Old Doc and the dozens of letters he had received from grateful patients.

4

Gottlieb Hoffmann

Gottlieb Hoffmann (we called him Gus) was one of my best friends. He was also my brother-in-law – that is to say, the husband of my wife's sister Ute (Inge).

Gottlieb was born in or near a town now called Sukhuvate, which had various name changes over the past century. It was also part of different countries, from Romania, to Bessarabia, to the Moldavian S.S.R., and it may now be part of the Ukraine – or, at least, very close to the Ukraine – considering the relocated Ukrainian borders. When Gottlieb was born, in the early 1930s[4], Sukhuvate's name may have been Kurudschika, but one would have to do more in-depth research or visit the place to get the exact history.

Gottlieb came to Canada in 1952. I first met him in August 1953 at Progress Electric Ltd., where we both served our apprenticeship as electricians. Our friendship started immediately after we met and lasted all through the years until Gottlieb died in August 2007.

During our apprenticeship with Progress Electric, Gottlieb and I attended technical school twice together

---

[4] Gottlieb always wondered when, exactly, he was born. Both his father and his mother disagreed on the year and the month of his birth date. Gottlieb eventually decided on November 16th 1931, but for all he knew, the date could well have been some time in December 1932. A date in Eastern Europe becomes even more muddled if one does not know which calendar, the Julian or the Gregorian, was used to establish the date.

in Calgary. Those were exciting times for us. At the end of our apprenticeship, we attended technical school for three months. We roomed together and spent a good deal of time exploring southern Alberta. Our favorite places were the mountains west of Calgary and the bathing pools fed by hot sulfur springs in or near Banff. After we wrote our final year's technical school examinations in June, 1957, we decided to take what we considered a "well-deserved" vacation – that is, a six-week trip to eleven western states of the USA, returning to Alberta via British Columbia.

We left Edmonton on the second of July, taking Gottlieb's brand new Ford Meteor Rideau car for this trip rather than my old 1948 Chevy. On the first day, we drove through Calgary, down to Cardston, and across the US border into Montana. We were trying to reach Great Falls on the first day; however, a retired sheriff sideswiped our car about 3.5 miles south of St. Mary. He panicked and stepped on the gas instead of the brakes and hit a boat trailer pulled by a car in front of him. The impact threw the boat trailer into the opposite lane, stopped another car, which caused a rear-end collision of yet another car.

We had stopped to watch the pile-up behind us in horror. The retired sheriff ran back to us with a drawn revolver in his hand, yelling something unintelligible. Luckily, we were able to take a picture of our tire track, which went through the dirt that had dropped from the sideswiped fender; this was definite proof that he hit us on our side of the solid line on the road.

♣

Nevertheless, the sheriff from Babb asked us to stay overnight at a nearby motel, because he wanted us to follow him to Cut Bank the next morning to make a statement to the Highway Patrol.

After the Highway Patrol cleared us, we took two days to enjoy ourselves around Great Falls. Then, we pushed on to the Yellowstone Park in Wyoming and to Idaho Falls in Idaho. We stopped in Salt Lake City, Utah, for a short visit with the Weidman family, my mother's friends from Berlin. Next, we drove to Arizona to visit the Grand Canyon and then to Las Vegas, Nevada, where each of us lost $50.00 of our hard-earned and/or borrowed money – about ten percent of the money we had budgeted for this six-week trip!

Naturally, we were reluctant to give up on our losses. At that time, we were still sure we could beat the odds that favored the house, using a simple method just doubling our bets after each loss, but we decided to phone a friend in Los Angeles, Gordon Michie, and ask him for his advice. "Cut your losses and get out of there as soon as possible," was his recommendation. "You cannot beat the odds in the long run – maybe not even in the short run!"

So, we packed up and continued on our way south, following the Colorado River to Blythe, California. We felt like we were driving through a furnace. The temperature had reached 120° F, and the air around us literally quivered. We soon spotted a beautiful, blue lake to the west of us – a welcome sight. We wasted no time trying to reach it, to no avail, and we finally realized that it was only a mirage.

We stayed overnight in Blythe. After an early breakfast next morning, we found a court summons under our windshield wiper. Apparently, we had parked the car in a prohibited zone after midnight. We dropped in at the Highway Patrol station, and the officer in charge graciously allowed us to pay the penalty to save us the trouble of returning to appear in court. He also warned us to be careful on the highway to Los Angeles. Apparently, two Canadians had been killed a few days earlier – squashed between two semis. We thanked him and were on our way west.

The road west of Blythe can only be compared to a roller coaster. In less than half an hour, we ended up between two semis, and the roller-coaster road condition made it impossible to pass the semi in front of us. We were glad when we were able to turn off at Palm Springs to have an early lunch. It was too early to stop at Gordon's house in Baldwin Park, a suburb of Los Angeles, so we drove through Los Angeles to Santa Monica Beach for an afternoon of relaxation. We arrived at Gordon's house just before supper, and Kay, his wife, gave us a warm welcome and invited us to stay with them for a while. We thanked her and ended up staying more than two weeks.

Next morning, when we went outside for our sunrise exercise before breakfast, we were amazed to see some mountains to the north – the San Gabriel Mountains. They were not visible the day before. Gordon told us that there had been too much smog to see them. It was Sunday, a day of rest for Gordon and

Kay, and we decided to join them and their children on a trip to Huntington Beach. However, too many oil wells were scattered along the beach to enjoy ourselves thoroughly, and we told the Michies that we preferred Santa Monica Beach.

During the next five days, while Gordon was working, Gottlieb and I did a lot of sightseeing. We spent some time in Los Angeles and Disneyland, and ended up at Long Beach, photographing the Miss Universe contestants. Gottlieb used a very impressive, Swiss-made, Bolex movie camera, and my German-made 35mm camera looked professional as well. So, being mistaken for members of the press, we had no trouble getting close to most of the contestants.

For the coming weekend, Gottlieb and I planned to take a run down to Mexico. Gordon decided to join us. We only got as far as Tijuana, and, mistakenly, we judged all of Mexico by this town. Our photographic exploits were very much unappreciated in Tijuana, especially in the residential district. After midnight, we decided to head back to San Diego. The Mexican custom official just waved us through, but we had a problem at the USA customs office. Gottlieb had obtained a single-entry visa to the United States in Canada, and the customs' official considered the reentry from Mexico a second entry. We argued that we had assumed the single entry applied only Canada, but the customs' official did not buy it. Then we started pleading with him. Gottlieb said that we were only there (in Mexico) for a day's visit, and he pointed to his car, which was sitting in a nearby parking lot on the US side of the border. The customs' official finally relented and let us pass, but giving us a stern lecture to be more careful in the future, which we faithfully promised him to be. We breathed a sigh of relief to be back in the United States.

We stayed overnight in San Diego and then drove back to Gordon and Kay's home, via the California dessert and along the Salton Sea, which lies 250 feet below sea level. During the next few days, we spent some time swimming and sunning at the Santa Monica Beach, shopping in Los Angeles, and sightseeing in Hollywood. On our second-last evening with Gordon and Kay, we took them to a show and a swanky restaurant in Hollywood for a steak dinner. On the last evening with them, we played bridge. Kay and I partnered. She was worried and asked me not to bawl her out if she made any mistakes. "I won't," I assured her (apprehensively). She and I lost, of course.

Next morning, we headed north, taking the coastal highway. We took our time sightseeing and enjoyed the awesome views along Big Sur. To this day, my only regret is that I didn't stop to see Henry Miller in Big Sur. He had settled in Big Sur in 1944. Henry Miller is one of my favorite authors, and I had missed an excellent opportunity to shake his hand.

We stopped in Monterey for the night and then proceeded to San Francisco, stopping briefly in Santa Cruz to admire, with amazement, their famous mystery spot. We stayed five days in San Francisco, which has an atmosphere all of its own. The city comes close to European cities.

Gottlieb Hoffmann

♣

We enjoyed the peace in Golden Gate Park, the meals at Fishermen's Wharf, the hustle and bustle in China Town, the Irish coffees at the Buena Vista, and the curio shopping along Market Street.

One hot afternoon, Gottlieb and I were sitting in a downtown bar enjoying a couple of glasses of beer. Two tables down from us were two young women giving us some speculative looks. On the spur of the moment, Gottlieb asked them if they would like to join us at our table. They readily agreed and brought their glasses over. For half an hour, we discussed various points of interest in the San Francisco area – they were supplying us with a few interesting historical particulars. But, when Gottlieb started to make some complimentary personal remarks to them, and I saw the amorous look in his eyes, I decided to change the subject. I told them of some fictitious, hair-raising, adventures that involved Gottlieb and me. At first, they thought I was joking. I had to add more realism to my stories, until I detected a fearful look in their eyes. Then, they remembered they were late for an appointment. They got up suddenly, wished us well, and left. "Why did you scare them off like that?" Gottlieb wanted to know in an accusatory tone. "I didn't want us to get too chummy with them, Gus. We have to think of our girlfriends back home, you know." He just shook his head in disgust, but didn't contradict me.

We left San Francisco across the Golden Gate Bridge and proceeded again along the coastal highway, first to Eureka and then to Astoria.

We were eyeing the sun in San Francisco, hoping it would be with us for a while, but we didn't see it again until we returned to Alberta!

We stopped frequently at points of interest. Farther north, we stopped at Port Angeles, where we had to make a serious decision: Do we take the ferries to reach Vancouver via Victoria and Swartz Bay, or do we drive to Vancouver via Seattle and White Rock? We decided to drive. Before we reached Vancouver, we stopped at Matsqui to pick up Siegfried (Fred) Friedrich, a friend of ours who stayed at my Aunt Dorathea's twin sister Lilly's farm. Fred had also been an apprentice at Progress Electric, but had decided to leave Edmonton and settle in the Vancouver area. For the next three days, the three of us explored Vancouver and Mission City. Fred was already familiar with many points of interest. We had a good time together.

Gottlieb Hoffmann

♣

In Oregon, Gottlieb
casts a yearning
look at the ocean –
missing the sun.

On August 9th, Gottlieb and I left Matsqui, Fred, and the coastal region and drove into the interior of British Columbia. We followed the Frazer River for a while and then drove through the Cascades to Kimberly, where we stayed overnight. Ever since we had left San Francisco, we yearned for sunshine. We finally got our wish when we left the mountains on our way to Calgary. Both of us were so elated that we promised each other to make Alberta our home base.

In Calgary, we paid a visit to Hans and Helga Hohenwarter and stayed with them for a day. Helga had been my girlfriend in Berlin. Now she was married to Hans and I was on my way to see my new girlfriend, Renate Sowa. Hans was a lot of fun. As soon as we entered their house in Calgary, Hans offered us a cool beer and started the barbeque.

Gottlieb's sister, Leni, was the first one to welcome us back in Edmonton, after our trip to the States.

That evening, we sat up well past midnight reminiscing about times past. In the morning, Hans served us a cool beer – to prevent a hangover, as he put it – and a breakfast consisting of French bread and escargots in their original shell swimming in melted garlic butter. He made some jokes that they were still alive, which gave Helga the shivers. We had such a good time that we almost extended our stay, but we were on our way to Edmonton by noon. The first one to greet us back home was Leni, Gottlieb's sister.

Our trip together to the USA was, somehow, the end of an era for Gottlieb and me. Henceforth, we spent more time with our new girlfriends, whom we had befriended during the previous New Year's party at Klaus and Sigi Glimski's house. Two of Sigi's sisters, Renate and Inge, who had arrived from Germany in the fall, stayed at their house. For Gottlieb and me, meeting them was truly love-at-first-sight, for him with Inge, and for me with Renate.

In the spring following our return from the States, I invited Gottlieb and Inge to join Renate and me on a hike up a mountain in Jasper Park. When we reached the top, I proposed to Renate and gave her a ring to make her my fiancée. Gottlieb and Inge were more excited than Renate and I, I think. They had never heard of anyone proposing to his sweetheart on top of a mountain. Renate and I got married in November 1958, and Gottlieb and Inge got married in August 1959.

The four of us loved the outdoors and went on many camping and fishing trips together. One summer, we started out on a fishing trip near Rocky Mountain House. We tried fishing for brown trout, but Gottlieb was the only one of us to catch this wary fish. At our campfire that evening, he made sure we knew what we were doing wrong. Nevertheless, we talked him into driving farther west, to Nordegg, where we knew the fish were easier to catch. So, on the next day, we moved our camp to Goldeye Lake.

Gottlieb decided to fish the lake at sunrise, while the rest of us took our time getting up and eating our breakfast. We were leisurely drinking our coffees, watching Gottlieb trying to catch some fish.

Well past ten o'clock, I finally called to Gottlieb to come and pick me up. In the boat, I took my time rigging up some salmon-egg cluster, which I dropped over the side, just where the lake bottom dropped off to unknown depth. Still, I had to be patient until noon to catch my first fish. Immediately, I felt that I had a big one on the line. He bent my rod u-shaped, and tightened my six-pound line close to breaking point. The trout jumped several times out of the water, trying to shake the hook. He fought valiantly for about forty minutes, but I finally netted him – a big rainbow trout, weighing almost seven pounds.

Gottlieb was audibly upset. "I'm already out here for several hours, since early morning, trying in vain to catch some fish," he complained, "and you come out in the middle of the day and catch this granddaddy."

Yes, I did, but I kept my mouth shut. Nothing is served by rubbing it in. When he glared at me for a while, I felt obligated to sooth him a little: "Just dumb luck, Gus."

The four of us fervently devoured trout steaks that evening, at our campfire, together with fried fresh mushrooms, which the women had picked in the afternoon, and with a bottle of cool Winzertanz wine. We stayed at Goldeye Lake a few more days, at Gottlieb's insistence, unsuccessfully trying to catch another granddaddy. Finally, Gottlieb got impatient and said, "Let's drive to Wildhorse Lake. Maybe we'll have more luck there. We'll take the David Thompson Trail."

The David Thompson Trail was still a primitive track at that time, without bridges over mountain streams. The trail was very different from today's David Thompson Highway. We had taken Gottlieb's

♣

Mercedes, which had a powerful diesel engine, yet, we had our problems negotiating the rough terrain. At one point, Gottlieb got stuck half way up a hill, and Renate, Inge, and I had to get out of the car and help push it all the way up. At another time, Gottlieb was stuck in the middle of a stream. He backed the car out again. Gottlieb and I waded into the stream to remove an obstructive rock. While we were busy doing so, a wasp stung Gottlieb close to his left eye, which instantly swelled shut. We applied some bite soother, but the swelling remained for two more days. We also ran into momma bears with cubs, and kept ourselves well within the car for protection.

At a campground near Hinton, Gottlieb and I decided to fish Wildhorse Lake from shore. We parked the car at an abandoned camp on the east side of the lake and walked along a foot trail a few hundred yards along the wooded shore to find an ideal spot from where to cast our lines and lures. The rainbow trout we were catching weren't big, probably one to one-and-a-half pounds, but we had fun catching them. We were close to our catch-limit when we saw a brown bear coming at us, still two hundred yards away. We reeled in our lines, packed up, and started to run back around the lake, but the brown bear steadily gained some distance on us. We decided to leave him a few fish on the trail, but it hardly slowed him down. However, we finally reached Gottlieb's car with only a few yards between the bear and us. As Gottlieb started his diesel engine, the engine's loud tractor-noise scared the bear off. He gave an angry grunt, immediately turned around, and hightailed his way back. "That was a close call," I told Gottlieb. We both heaved a big sigh of relief. Safely back in camp, we were telling our wives how a big brown bear almost mauled us. Inge said, "I can hardly believe that you were able to outrun the brown bear. Brown bears are known to be fast runners." I smiled and explained to her that we had gladly offered him some of our catch to slow him down. We had another trout dinner that evening and discussed adverse possibilities of our experience well into the night.

The four of us, and later together with our children, continued to go on adventurous camping and fishing trips for many years.

Gottlieb and I also wanted to sail. We took some sailing lessons and looked around for boats. I found a Solo and bought it. Gottlieb decided to build his own boat. We spent many winter evenings building it. Eventually, I sold my Solo. It proved to be too much for me, storing it for the winter, etcetera.

They told me that a sailor's happiest days are the day he buys his boat and the day he sells his boat. That was certainly true in my case, but Gottlieb and I had a few happy days as well, sailing it.

Gottlieb Hoffmann

♣

Rudy Hoffmann, myself, and Gottlieb on a duck-hunting trip.

Gottlieb and I were also devoted hunters – mainly bird hunters. We hunted frequently with Gottlieb's brother Rudy. Rudy was a few years older than Gottlieb, and we appreciated his hunting tips. He was also what they commonly call a crack shot, and, with him along on hunting trips, we seldom came home without our limit. Gottlieb and I were mere tyros compared to Rudy.

Besides camping, fishing, and hunting, Gottlieb and I liked throwing parties. We had a circle of friends who felt likewise, and we never missed a good reason for having a party. Our parties included outdoor barbeques as well. Sometimes we had these barbeques in one of our backyards and, at other times, we had them at a nearby lake. Our indoor parties would also include dance music. Gottlieb and Inge loved to jive, and Renate and I loved to tango. To watch Gottlieb jive was an awesome affair. He rolled Inge across his back during his acrobatic maneuvers as if she were merely a handball. Renate's and my tango dances were sedate in comparison.

Gottlieb and I are enjoying a glass of my homemade wine together.

On winter days, when we did not go skiing or ice fishing, we played games. Our favorite game was Stock Ticker. Gottlieb and I enjoyed the game for its educational value, because we were also investing our spare cash in the real market, but our wives enjoyed the game for its own sake. We also formed a private skat club. Skat is the German equivalent game to the

English whist or bridge games, except that men rather than women favor it more. So, whenever our club buddies met to play skat, the women usually played Scrabble or Monopoly.

We amply recorded all of our trips and parties and dances on film, since Gottlieb and I were both ardent photographers. We had the prevailing state-of-the-art cameras and camera accessories, and we took hundreds of feet of movies and hundreds of still pictures to show off our photographic skills.

The 1970s brought some significant changes to our lives. Rudy passed away suddenly, and we lost interest in our hunting trips. In addition, I had less time available, because I took on the responsibilities of a trustee for health & welfare and pension trust funds. In 1975, the Edmonton electricians went on strike, and Gottlieb decided to start a nonunion company. Then, in 1979, Vic Webb, the owner of Progress Electric, started negotiations with a Quebec company to buy him out. He sold his company a year later.

In 1984, Gottlieb and Inge moved to Kelowna, British Columbia. After that, we saw less of each other. Gottlieb also developed a dangerous habit of drinking by himself.

One morning, shortly after midnight, my phone rang. Gottlieb was on the line, sounding frantic: "You have to help me, Art. Inge left me!"

I was stunned: "What happened?"

"She got fed up with my drinking habits," he wailed. I knew that his drinking problem had got worse, but I was under the impression that Inge had convinced him to join the AA. "I can't live without Inge," Gottlieb sobbed. He was genuinely crying. "What can I do to get her back, Art?"

I was still a little sleep groggy. After a few seconds, I said, "The first thing you should do, Gus, is don't touch another drink for as long as you live. Do you think you can do that?"

"I'll do anything to get Inge back, but I don't think she'll believe me."

"You'll have to sincerely try to convince her, somehow."

"Will you talk to her, Art?"

"I'll talk to her, but you'll have to follow through on your promise, Gus."

"I'll do that – I swear!"

"Okay. Where is she now?"

"I think she went to Dacy's." Dacy is their eldest daughter.

"I'll call Dacy and get back to you," I said.

"Thanks. You're the only friend I can depend on."

I talked to Inge, but she was not receptive to any reconciliation. She told me that she was afraid of Gottlieb, that he had threatened her with a gun. It took me a few more days to convince her to return to Gottlieb. Of course, he didn't keep his promise, but Inge remained with him anyway.

One time, when Renate and I were visiting them in Kelowna, he told me, in private, "If I can't drink anymore, Art, I might as well die." At the time, I had no idea how true that prediction would turn out to be.

Gottlieb and I sit in deep meditation amidst our beloved wilderness.

A few weeks before Gottlieb died, he called me in a maudlin mood. He said he was all alone and had reread my poem book. "I really like your poem *Their Leader*, and I wrote a tune for it. Do you mind?"

Mind? Why should I if it made him feel good? Gottlieb played the piano, but his favorite instrument was the accordion.

"Of course, I don't mind!" I assured him.

I called him just one week prior to his death. He was in good spirits but sounded a little sick to me. A foreboding made me call Inge and ask her if I should fly out to see him, but she discouraged me from doing so. Neither of us expected him to die so soon.

Nevertheless, Gottlieb did die soon after my telephone call, on August 3ʳᵈ 2007, and Inge arranged the funeral for August 13th, a date shortly before my attendance of a trustees' conference in Chicago. However, Renate and I decided to fly to Kelowna first to pay our last respects to Gottlieb and to empathize with his immediate family. This trip turned out to be full of surprises for us.

We stayed at Max and Barb's house. (Barbara is Renate's youngest sister.) Leni and Albert Lehmann, her husband, had flown in from Waterloo, Ontario, and stayed at Max and Barb's as well. I was surprised how little Leni and Albert had changed in all these years, and, despite the sadness of the occasion, we were happy to see each other again. We immediately resumed an old friendship.

At the funeral, a picture gallery was on display – perhaps a couple of hundred pictures. Renate mentioned later that she saw only one picture[5] with Gottlieb and me in it: a small group picture of a few Progress Electric employees. She found this omission strange, considering the amount of time Gottlieb and I and our families had spent together over the years. Who knows? Perhaps Inge had nothing to do with selecting these pictures. Perhaps her children, who had less awareness of our closeness, especially during our earlier years together, selected the pictures. However, it made me even sadder to lose Gottlieb.

Another surprise was meeting Freda Madsen again. Freda is one of Gottlieb's cousins. After her first husband died, she married Gordon Hammond, a good

---

[5] Gottlieb's son, David, told me later that there were more pictures of Gottlieb and me displayed. I'll take his word for it, because Renate did not see any more.

friend of mine. Gordon and I had joked about the coincidence of becoming remote relatives through marriage. However, Freda and Gordon separated soon after their marriage. I had written a sad poem about their unhappiness, which is included in my poem book. I mentioned this to Freda, and she expressed the desire to receive a copy of the book, which I mailed to her after my return from Chicago.

Leni, too, asked me to send her a copy of the poem book, as well as my storybook called *Trials and Errors, Laughs and Terrors.* I had told her that the storybook contains some adventure stories involving Gottlieb and her late brother Rudy, although I have changed the names. I managed to mail these two books to Leni before I left for Chicago. While Renate and I were in Chicago, Nancy, my daughter, relayed to us a message from Leni. Not only did she express her own delight about the books, but she also requested another poem book for a German lady who was visiting them at that time and who liked the poems so much that she started copying them out of Leni's book. Naturally, I mailed off another book immediately upon my return to Edmonton and was glad to hear that it reached this woman before her return to Germany.

One last surprise I received while we were in Kelowna was a chastising by my brother-in-law Max. Max and I were never close friends, but we maintained an amicable relationship over the years. He complained that we never invite them to our house anymore. We used to have parties regularly at our house – mostly birthday parties. Now, he protested, we invite them to restaurants when he and Barb come to Edmonton and express the desire to get together.

"I will never eat at restaurants," he made clear to me, "I prefer home cooking anytime!"

I tried to explain to him that most of the time our living room is in a mess, what with all the papers I receive as a trustee, which I filed away neatly when I still had an office.

"I don't care about that," he cried, "I come to see you, not your papers!"

Well, what could I do? I sincerely apologized to him and promised to invite him to my messy house next time he and Barbara come to Edmonton.

Overall, the funeral was a success, if that is the right word to use for a funeral, but I still miss my old friend Gottlieb dearly. As I told my daughter Nancy at one time, not all the wealth in the world replaces the loss of one good friend!

5

Anton Sowa

Anton Sowa was my father-in-law. I couldn't have wished for a better one. He and his wife, my mother-in-law, paid us their first visit in 1966 – eight years after my wife, Renate, and I were married. They had arrived just before Christmas, and, as expected, we celebrated Christmas German-style, including a roasted goose, raw potato dumplings, red cabbage, and Winzertanz, an excellent, German white wine.

Renate called him Vati, pronounced "fahtee," and, soon, I got into the same habit. Sons-in-law are usually hesitant about calling their fathers-in-law by an intimate father title, but he made me feel so welcome and so much like his own son that I never gave the matter a second thought. In fact, I felt like I had known him all my life. Her mother, Renate called Mutti, with the "i" pronounced "ee" and the "u" pronounced as in "put."

Shortly into the New Year, 1967, we picked a nice, sunny day to pay a visit to my folks in the Barrhead area. (Barrhead is about 120 km northwest of Edmonton.) Although the temperature had dropped down to -30°C, we trusted my American Motor's Ambassador (sedan) car to get us there and back.

My folks were almost overenthusiastic to have visitors from Germany, especially on such a cold day, and coffee, cakes, wine, and other spirits came in a

Arthur O.R. Thormann

♣

steady supply throughout our visit.

There was much to talk about, of course, and when I suggested getting ready to leave, my folks and my in-laws took another hour to let me convince them to postpone any further conversation. All during their chattering, I had cast worried looks outside. Snow had begun to fall, and a wind was starting to blow. Blizzards in Canada can be traumatic at the best of times, and I did not want to risk a breakdown in the middle of nowhere.

When we finally said our good-byes, late afternoon, we had about an hour of daylight left – only half as much as I would have liked to have. Visibility on the highway was limited to about 50 meters and getting less by the minute. I drove as fast as road and weather conditions allowed, which was about half our speed in the morning. We were roughly 50 km from Edmonton when I heard a loud racket at the right rear fender. I stopped the car immediately and got out to inspect the damage. Vati rolled down a window and asked me what was wrong.

"I don't know yet," I said. "I'm going to put a blanket on the ground and have a look underneath."

He climbed out of the car immediately to lend me a hand. I took an old blanket out of the trunk, spread it on the ground near the right rear fender, and got down on it to look behind the tire. In the beam of my flashlight, I could see that the piston rod of the shock absorber had come off its mount and had extended out to poke into the tire. I tried to move it, but it was jammed tight. I got up and informed Vati of the

52

problem. "We can't continue home this way," I said. He gave me a worried look. The temperature had dropped a little after sundown, and he was probably concerned about the women and children – we had our two daughters with us.

Vati and I debated for a few minutes what would be the best action. I knew the nearest village was about eight kilometers away, but I dreaded the walk there in this blizzard. On the other hand, we could not wait out the blizzard in the car too long, with the motor running. Sometimes, especially during very cold temperatures, it is almost as if one's brain is frozen. We finally decided to flag down a passing car and depend on the driver to send help back to us. Remember: This was in the pre-cell-phone days.

We did not have long to wait. Another driver stopped behind us, got out, introduced himself, and enquired about our problem. I told him briefly what was wrong, and he promptly went back to his trunk and returned with a toolbox. He picked out a small socket, a ratchet wrench, and an extension long enough to reach the nut he was trying to loosen. He asked me to get the jack out of my trunk and promptly jacked up the right side of my car. Then, he got down on the ground, took my flashlight, fiddled around for a while, and stood back up with the culprit shock absorber in his hand. At my astonished look, he explained that he was a mechanic.

"Drive slowly and avoid potholes," he said, "and you'll be okay." Thankfully, I offered him some money, but he declined it.

♣

On the rest of the way home, Vati explained to the women what had happened. He went on and on about the helpfulness and selflessness of the mechanic. It took us another hour to get home. After we removed our winter coats, I poured us all a stiff drink and Vati raised his glass and said, "Na denn!" – "Well, then!" This was a favorite expression he used when imbibing alcoholic spirits.

On the following weekend, Vati and I looked up the mechanic's address and delivered to him a bottle of whiskey, which he gladly accepted.

Soon afterwards, Vati and Mutti decided to ride out the Canadian winter in California, where their oldest daughter lived. Renate and I promised to come and pick them up in May and drive them back to Canada.

To keep our promise, I took a two-week vacation, which gave us seventeen days for the trip to California, including Victoria Day. We decided to take our camping equipment along. It took us all of three days to reach San Jose, where Renate's sister Sigrid and her husband Klaus lived. Their house was large enough to put all of us up for a few days, and Sigrid was an excellent hostess. Horst, Klaus's cousin, and his wife, Maudi, who lived in Oakland, came to visit us nearly everyday, and, together, we went on various excursion trips.

One day, during a shopping trip to San Francisco, Maudi talked us into having a Chinese lunch. We picked an authentic looking Chinese restaurant in San

Francisco's Chinatown and sat down at a large round table with a Lazy Susan.

Vati was sitting on my left studying his menu. "I wonder if they serve hamburgers here," he mumbled.

"Ask the waiter," I suggested.

After the waiter placed a huge pot of Chinese tea and ten tiny cups on the Lazy Susan, Vati looked at him and said, "Hamburger?" The waiter looked dismayed and gesticulated wildly, pointing at another restaurant across the street. Vati thought that the waiter had misunderstood him and repeated louder, "Hamburger!"

The waiter, whose English language was insufficient to express his dismay, cried something unintelligible, and Maudi, who did not want to leave for another restaurant, offered her help. She told Vati that she would order for him the Chinese equivalent of hamburger. Vati nodded. He was satisfied.

We started with soup – won ton soup. I could see on Vati's expression that he liked the soup. He probably compared it to hamburger, no doubt. As the waiter served the main course, he put a huge bowl of more won ton soup in front of Vati. "War won ton," Maudi mimicked to me from across the table. I smiled.

Now it was Vati's turn to object. He waved his hands in a "stop" fashion and said to the waiter, "No, no! I've had enough soup!"

The waiter gave Maudi a helpless look, and Maudi turned to Vati and said, "This is your hamburger."

Vati wailed, "But I don't want any more soup! I

want some real hamburger!"

Maudi explained patiently, "This is the closest to hamburger they have here, Vati."

Vati just shook his head and stared at this huge bowl of more won ton soup.

I felt sorry for him. "Tomorrow we'll go and have some real hamburger," I promised him.

He was silent for a while. Finally, he fished out three or four more dumplings from this huge bowl and then abandoned the rest of it. This was the last time in California that we talked him into going to a Chinese restaurant.

After we left the restaurant and walked down the street toward the wharf, Vati suddenly tugged my sleeve and pulled me to the curb, to avoid my walking under a ladder placed on the sidewalk by a tradesman.

"Bad luck!" He said.

His generation was more prone to superstition than ours was. Perhaps this was the reason why he was unwilling to eat Chinese food. He also disliked other food, like tomatoes, for instance. He called them "rheuma" apples, probably implying that tomatoes caused rheumatism.

On most days, we just went sightseeing and shopping. However, one day we decided to go deep-sea fishing. We drove to San Francisco and chartered a boat. I think the captain of the chartered boat promised us some salmon activity. I cannot remember now if we actually caught any fish, but we had a great time trying. Somewhere along the coast, we saw a grounded concrete ship. Horst told us a detailed history of these ships, which the Kaiser shipyards near San Francisco had built during World War II.

On another day, Sigrid drove us to some vineyards, where we nearly got drunk tasting their various wines. Naturally, we also bought a few bottles for consumption during our evenings. In the evenings, we often played skat. Skat is a German, three handed card game, using thirty-two cards of the deck. Two players usually play in partnership against the player who won the bid. Klaus was very good at the game, because he played it regularly at the German club. However, Vati was not bad either. He and Mutti played it at home occasionally, with Mutti's brother. The game requires much logic and a good memory for the cards previously played, and a player who makes a mistake is usually criticized by his/her partner. Nevertheless, we had a lot of fun playing the game and drinking our California wines.

On the eve before our departure, Sigrid invited some neighbors and friends for a going-away bash. Her intentions were well meant, I'm sure, but I would have preferred a more quiet evening and going earlier to bed. We got up early the next morning, had a brief breakfast, and then headed north, taking the more scenic coastal highway.

We stopped frequently at points of interest. Along the Oregon coast, Vati decided to dive into the high ocean waves that pounded the shoreline. We just sat in the car watching him and admiring his gumption.

As we crossed the border into Canada, I showed my driver's license to the customs' official without getting out of the car. He looked at Renate and the children in the front seat and asked me if we were all Canadians. I just nodded, and he waved us on. Soon after we left the border, I realized that this didn't apply to Vati and Mutti, but we were already too far into Canada to turn around to correct things. However, later, my mistake caused Vati and Mutti a problem when they were leaving Canada for Europe, because their papers did not indicate to show if, and when, they had left the United States.

Back in Edmonton, we naturally had to have another party with all the relatives to celebrate our return. Vati and Mutti had lots to talk about, and, with the assistance of California wine and Greek brandy, we made a few grand plans for fishing and camping trips during the upcoming three summer months – giving Vati detailed and exaggerated descriptions of past conquests.

One Sunday afternoon, Renate decided to bake a few cakes for her birthday party the following Wednesday. It was a hot summer day, and the baking turned the whole kitchen into an oven. Naturally, Renate was complaining about the heat. Vati and I were in the living room, reading. Finally, I had heard enough of Renate's complaining, and I asked her why not simply buy some cake at the German bakery.

When Mutti heard this comment, she flew out of her bedroom like a hawk and yelled at me not to insult her daughter. "How can you even suggest that a bakery's cake compares to my daughter's baking?" she cried.

I tried to explain to her that we frequently bought cake at the German bakery, and that the cake is very good, but the more I said, the more excited she became, until we were engaged in an out-and-out altercation. I finally told her, "I might as well move out of my own house if I'm not allowed to make any suggestions!" With these words, I stormed out of the front door.

Vati, who had pretended to read a magazine while I had this row with Mutti, followed me. We walked silently together for ten minutes. Then he said to me, "You were slightly off base." He meant this about some of the things I had said to his wife. It was the only criticism I remember ever receiving from him. "The wiser one gives in," he added.

I nodded. Of course, he was right, and I suddenly felt ashamed of my conduct. We continued walking in silence for another half an hour. When we got back to the house, I went straight to Mutti's room and apologized for my behavior. At first, she looked at me suspiciously, but when she saw that I meant what I said, she smiled slightly and wagged her forefinger at me: "You must never insult my daughter's cooking or baking," she whispered warningly. I just nodded. The wiser one gives in! This is a very valuable piece of advice, which helped me past many a rough spot over the following years.

Mutti and I hugged each other. We were both glad about the successful conclusion. That was the last time I remember having had an altercation with her.

When I returned to the living room, Vati was still pretending to be engrossed in his magazine. He had a hint of a smile on his face, as if he had just read something humorous. Then he looked up at me and nodded his approval. That had meant a lot to me.

I watched Vati's interaction with the grandchildren many times. By the time of their first visit with us, Vati and Mutti had all of ten grandchildren. Vati was kind to them and gave them gifts, but he was also strict with them. They did not seem to mind. They respected him. I mentioned this to him one time and asked him what his secret was. He said, "Children are like little adults, and I treat them as such. I treat them like I would treat adults who require some training, and they appreciate that."

This comment changed my own behavior with children. Up to that point, I had always treated children as some inferior beings. I had honestly not thought of children as "little adults." It made a whale of a difference in my life to look at and treat children as little adults, and soon I, too, started earning their respect.

Vati used most of his spare time to produce a few paintings for us. He was not so much an original painter as he was a copycat, but he was good at it – he definitely had an eye for colors. To copy an old master, he would take a postcard or a photograph from an art book and mark it up with vertical and horizontal gridlines, about one centimeter apart. He would also draw gridlines on his canvas. If the size of the painting was six times that of the postcard or photograph, he would draw gridlines on his canvas six centimeters apart. Then he would pencil-draw the outline of his subjects onto the canvas, matching the subjects in the grid squares of the postcard or photograph. Thus, he made sure that the copy was proportional to the original. Next, he would add the color detail with his brush. Lastly, he would sign his own name and the year in the bottom right corner of the painting. I watched him a few times and was quite amazed by the simplicity of the process. However, I don't believe that I could ever hope to duplicate it. He was definitely a master in his own right.

One of the old masters I fell in love with was Eugène Delacroix. I liked his vivid colors and the violence portrayed in some of his paintings, which probably says something about my own feelings at that time. I selected one of Delacroix's lion hunt paintings from an art book and asked Vati to paint it for me. He was delighted to do so. When he was finished, I took the canvas to an Italian frame shop that employed artisans to hand-carve special frames. The owner of the shop was so enthralled with my Delacroix copy that he offered me $500 for it. I declined, of course, although $500 was a lot of money for me in 1967. Vati agreed with my rejection of the storeowner's offer. The demand for his paintings was so high that he would not have had the time to paint another one for me.

July 1967 was a busy month for us. To begin with, we had several parties to celebrate Canada's 100th birthday. Then we celebrated Renate's birthday. After that, we got ready for Klondike days. This was a big ten-day affair, or better, fair, in Edmonton. Everyone dressed up in old Klondike attire, and Renate and her sister Inge were busy sewing for the occasion, especially new outfits for Vati and Mutti and the children. Finally, we would stroll up and down the promenade along Jasper Avenue and pose for camera bugs. Back home, during the evenings, we would continue our celebrations in full Klondike attire and with good food and wine. Klondike days were a very distinctive experience for Vati and Mutti.

During August that year, Gottlieb, Inge's husband, and I used some of our holidays to go on camping trips. Again, this was a new experience for Vati and Mutti, and they couldn't have wished for better guides: By that time, Gottlieb and I had spent at least ten years together roaming the country, hunting, and fishing. We were usually "roughing" it on our camping trips, but, I must say, Vati was a good sport. We didn't just make trips to lakes near Edmonton but also to rivers in mountainous areas. No matter what we dished out for him, Vati never complained. He went along with everything as if he were our age and not thirty years older.

Hunting was another matter. We were mostly hunting birds: geese, ducks, and upland game, and our hunting parties usually consisted of three or four close friends: Gottlieb's brother Rudy, for example, was always a good hunting companion. When the hunting season opened in September, we were ready for it. As well, we had coached Vati suitably, with tall tales from our previous hunting trips. He had never hunted anything in his life, but he gladly participated in our enthusiasm. However, he was definitely ill at ease on our first hunting trip. We had given him a shotgun, a duck call, and some detailed instructions, but he conducted himself worse than a lost sentry would.

I think he just detested killing of any kind. On the other hand, our hunting trips were more social get-togethers than serious shoots, and Vati thoroughly enjoyed that part of our outings. He always wanted to prove to his sons-in-law that he was part of the gang – and he was!

I reflected a lot over Vati's nonviolent nature during the next few years. Oddly enough, it took me another five years to conclude that hunting – killing – was slowly destroying my character, if not my soul, and I stopped the practice. Eventually, I sold all of my guns for less than half the price I had paid for them, but I was glad to get rid of their ominous existence near me.

All good things must come to an end, as the saying goes, and so it was with Vati and Mutti's visit. As we came closer to their departure, we increased our parties. Every one of their friends and relatives wanted to show some appreciation for their extended visit to us before they left, and throwing a party for them seemed the most appropriate action, since all of us could participate. Vati was in his element, of course, at these parties. He was quite a storyteller. I don't believe there was a subject on which he didn't know a suitable story. Most of his stories had a humorous aspect, and there was much laughter at these parties, which became louder with the consumption of wine and other spirits.

The last time I saw Vati was in July 1981. We had flown to Germany to celebrate Vati and Mutti's fiftieth wedding anniversary. Notwithstanding the festive mood, Vati seemed unusually solemn to me. I was very fond of him, and his serious disposition concerned me. One day, when Vati and I strolled through Borken, where they lived, he conveyed some strange, veiled messages to me, almost as if he didn't expect to live much longer. I didn't know what to make of his comments. Was it just a premonition on his part, or did he know something he wasn't telling us? He looked quite healthy to me, for an octogenarian, and he had no problems keeping up with my swift pace.

He must have seen the puzzled look on my face, because after a while he said, "Don't be sad, I've lived a full live." That comment really did worry me, and I put my right arm around his shoulders and gave him a gentle, empathetic squeeze. "You'll be with us for a long time yet," I assured him, as we continued our walk. He responded with a strange smile.

He died a year-and-a-half later, and I *was* sad – as I always am when a noble soul leaves our planet for the great beyond.

6

Edward Kriik

Edward Kriik (pronounced: "creek") was an Estonian electrician who lived and worked for a while in Sweden before he came to Canada. I think he arrived in 1949, because he told me once that his International Brotherhood of Electrical Workers' union membership started then. I first met him in August of 1953, when I started my electrician's apprenticeship at Progress Electric Ltd., where he worked as a foreman.

I will always remember Ed Kriik as a grumpy old man; nevertheless, he eventually became a good friend. Ed was a beer drinker, although he would not refuse wine or hard liquor either. During weekdays, we stopped in occasionally at some lounge to have a couple of glasses of beer and discuss the day's work problems.

My real companionship with Ed developed on weekends, when we went either fishing or hunting together. When I say "hunting together," I must clarify that Ed only came along for company; he adamantly refused to shoot at anything alive! However, he was an ardent angler and didn't mind killing the fish he caught. Gottlieb Hoffmann, who was Ed's apprentice, completed our trio of enthusiastic, and adventurous, I might add, anglers. We were an inseparable trio during our scores of philosophical discussion periods and on many exploratory fishing and hunting trips.

Laine and Ed Kriik, sitting ponderously in our garden.

Usually, our more adventurous trips took us to the Rocky Mountains on the Alberta side. One of our favorite haunts was the Wildhay River. In fact, it was at the Wildhay River where Gerry Woods, one of Northern Electric's salesmen, taught me how to fly fish. We fly-fished a lot along the Wildhay River, but the biggest fish we caught came from under the river's logjams. We sunk a lead weight into the water, between the logs, that had a dropper and a hook with salmon eggs attached to the line about a foot above the lead weight. The lead weight would lodge in the river's gravel bed, and the dropper with the salmon eggs would dance lively in the river's flowing water. The lure was irresistible to the wary trout. Nevertheless, we had plenty of time to philosophize between catches.

Edward Kriik

♣

Ed Kriik was my sounding board for philosophy. It started with his quotes of Latin terms. I still don't know where he acquired his knowledge of Latin, but he gave us his Latin wisdom for almost every topic we discussed. His Latin wisdom intrigued me so much that I went out to buy a dictionary on Latin terms and phrases.

Ed also knew his Bible. I remember one time when I showed him a new poem I had just typed up called *Enamored Buildings*. He read it slowly and then said, "You've made a mistake."

"What's that, Ed?"

"A rainbow didn't exist in the garden of Eden," he assured me.

He was referring to the poem lines: "It could have been the garden of Eden, except for the buildings." Along with the lines: "And in the midst of it all: the most beautiful rainbow: A rainbow only seen before in nature: never inside of buildings!"

I must have had a question mark on my face, because he went on to explain: "God created the rainbow after the deluge, as a token of His covenant with Noah and his sons: A sign that would appear as a reminder that God would not allow any more floods to occur. So, when you say: 'It could have been the garden of Eden…' this is not true if a rainbow is present."

I shook my head. He was right, of course. I had forgotten about God's covenant with Noah. However, I never changed the poem. In those days, I had the notion that I had written my poems because of some

67

inspiration and not because of reasoning and, therefore, they should remain as inspired.

At another time, I showed Ed a flattened penny that I had acquired recently in San Francisco, with the Lord's Prayer impressed on one side of it. It came from one of those cranking machines, where you insert a penny and select the picture or message you desire to be impressed on it, and then crank the penny through two steel rollers, similar to the two wooden rollers attached to old washing machines that removed most of the water from the washed clothing.

The flattened penny was oval shaped, large enough to hold the Lord's Prayer that I had selected to be impressed on it. Ed made sure all the words were there. Then he said, "I've always had some problems with this prayer."

"Oh? It seems pretty straight forward to me, Ed."

"That is what it's supposed to be, Art. Still, I have some problems with it."

"Give me an example."

"Well, take the line: 'Give us this day our daily bread.' That's like saying, 'Give me my pen (which you might have borrowed)."

"I don't believe that's a good comparison, Ed."

"Well, you're asking for something that's yours, but take another line: 'Forgive us our trespasses, as we forgive those who trespass against us.' With that wish, we wouldn't be forgiven many trespasses, would we?"

"You mean, because we're not very forgiving to those who trespass against us?"

"Yes, that's what I mean. The wish is conditional

on our forgiving others, which is not too often the case."

"Do you have any other examples?"

"Isn't that enough?"

"Well, I think those two examples could have different interpretations."

"Okay. How about this one: 'Lead us not into temptation.' I always thought that this was the job of the Devil – not God's doing. Furthermore, if you want yet another example, how about: 'Our Father, who art in heaven.' I always thought God is everywhere, not just in heaven."

I didn't have any good answers for Ed. We sat in silence for a while. I was rereading the Lord's Prayer on the flattened coin once more with Ed's comments in mind.

"There's one phrase here that *I* find very curious, Ed."

"What's that?"

"It says here, 'forever and ever.' That almost implies there's more after forever, that there is an end to forever."

Ed chuckled. "It's a well known misconception that the infinite is finite, that it's only a large number – even our dictionaries support such a notion. The idea of an end to forever may have existed already throughout history. So, I'm not surprised that Jesus added an 'ever' after 'forever' – perhaps, to give 'forever' more strength."

"I suppose so."

Nevertheless, Ed's comments on the Lord's

Prayer gave me something to think about for many years. I'm still not quite sure what to make of his observations, but, in the days when we had this discussion, I firmly believed that Jesus, who had first recommended the Lord's Prayer in His Sermon on the Mount, could do no wrong. However, after reading Bertrand Russell's essay *Why I Am Not A Christian*, I had to concede that Jesus was human in many ways, like the rest of us.

Ed and I were sitting on one of Wildhay River's log piles, jiggling our salmon eggs in the water. Gottlieb was a little further down stream fly-fishing, which he considered sportier. It was a clear, sunny day, the water was gurgling away beneath us, and we were musing about various subjects.

At one point, I asked, "Ed, can you be an atheist if you're an agnostic?"

"Why do you ask?"

"Well, I've been reading some of Bertrand Russell's material. He proclaimed to be an agnostic, but some of his assertions lead me to believe that he was actually an atheist."

"Atheism is the disbelief in the existence of God. Agnosticism merely believes that nothing is known, or knowable, of the existence of God."

"I know, but, if nothing is knowable of the existence of God, isn't that the same as disbelieving in the existence of God? What I mean is, if no evidence can be produced of the existence of God, wouldn't that lead one to disbelieve in the existence of God?"

"It could, I suppose, but philosophers still like to differentiate between agnosticism and atheism."

"Why, do you think, is that the case, Ed?"

"Perhaps in earlier days, it was less sinful to be an agnostic than to be an atheist," he laughed.

I shook my head. "I just can't believe that Bertrand Russell would have cared one way or the other, as he declared himself to be an agnostic. However, if he, indeed, believed in the nonexistence of God, I think he was wrong – from a philosophical viewpoint, I mean."

"What are you getting at, Art?"

"Okay, here's my reasoning: Can you think of anything that doesn't exist? If you can think of something, it must exist, even if only in your mind. That's what I'm getting at."

He pondered about this for a while. Then, he said, "I would have to agree with you – strictly from a philosophical viewpoint, mind you."

On that day, we never did settle these questions to our satisfaction; we merely added them as food for thought for future discussions.

At another time, we were sitting in a lounge enjoying a few glasses of beer, and I said to Ed, "Do you remember awhile back when we were discussing the 'forever' concept?"

"I do."

"What do you think of the old mathematician's belief that a number divided by zero yields infinity? Their reasoning was that when you divide a number by

Arthur O.R. Thormann

♣

a small fraction, you obtain a larger number, and the smaller the fraction the larger the number you obtain, until you reach zero as your divisor, which then yields the largest number of all: infinity."

"There's some logic in that belief."

"Well, our modern mathematicians do not think so. They tell us: You shall not divide by zero!"

"But that is to accommodate our mechanical and electrical calculators, which would try forever to find an answer to that division."

"I think there is a more profound explanation, Ed."

"What's that?"

"I think the explanation is that infinity is not a number at all, and a division always requires a number as an answer."

"Some of our dictionaries that define infinity as a huge number would disagree with you, Art. I think you know that."

"I do, but that doesn't change the fact that it's not a number."

"What's your explanation for that theory?"

"Simply this: A number is finite, and infinity is without end, in other words, not finite."

"I can't argue with that statement. I think I tried to make a similar point when we discussed the term 'forever' in the Lord's Prayer."

"You did, but I thought about it some more when I read in a 19th century German math book: $1/0 = \infty$."

Ed laughed. "What a confused, complex world we live in!"

72

Trout will not keep long without a fridge. Therefore, on camping trips, we kept only enough fish for supper each day, and on the last day, we took home our limit. Late afternoons, we abandoned the river's logjams and headed back to camp. We normally established our camp on the shore along the east side of Rock Lake. On the way to camp, we also picked a few mushrooms. We were very lucky to find the yellow boletus in the woods along the Wildhay River. It is one of the better mushrooms to eat. Fried fish and fried mushrooms provide an excellent meal in the wilderness.

After supper, we usually sat around the campfire, bragging about the day's catch. Gottlieb and I were smoking our brier pipes and Ed was enjoying a cigarillo. On cold evenings, we also made some hot toddies.

One evening, I looked up at the sky and exclaimed, "Man, will you look at those stars! There must be millions more to be seen here than back in the city."

"There are too many street lights in the city," observed Ed.

"Incidentally," I said, "did you guys read about that new UFO sighting in England?"

"Their imaginations seem to run wild over there," said Ed.

"Well, in any case, it makes you wonder, doesn't it? I mean, if there are UFOs, where could they come from?"

"Some other planetary system," said Gottlieb. "It's pretty well known that our planets cannot sustain

♣

life as we know it."

"Yes," I said, "but other planetary systems are much too far away."

"First of all," said Ed, "I don't believe that UFOs would sneak in and out of our environment without making official contact. Secondly, I agree with you, Art, that other planetary systems are too far away for the type of quick visits our UFO spotters report. However, if UFOs really exist, they wouldn't necessarily have to come from our planets or from other planetary systems."

"Then where else would they come from?" I enquired.

"Perhaps from one of Jupiter's moons," said Ed. "We really don't know too much about these moons. It's quite possible that one or more of them may have a life-sustaining environment, similar to ours on Earth."

Both Gottlieb and I were dumbfounded. This was news to us. "Have you read that somewhere, Ed?" I asked him.

"No. I was just thinking of nearer places rather than of other stars and planetary systems."

We were smoking away in silence for a while, sipping our hot toddies. Then, I broke the silence: "I'm still amazed by the number of stars out there. There must be millions if not billions out there! I wonder, sometimes, if there is an end to our universe."

"You may come to the end of our star system," said Ed, "but I doubt if you'll ever come to the end of the universe."

"You mean we could be looking at infinite

space?" I wanted to know.

"Yes, unless our universe is circular."

"What do you mean by circular?"

"Either a huge globe, perhaps adjoining other huge globes, or simply donut shaped."

"If the universe is donut shaped, where would you find the hole in the donut?" I asked.

"We've heard of black holes; that could be it."

There was silence again for a while, as we sat there thinking fantastic thoughts. Then, Gottlieb wanted to know, "If UFOs do come from other planetary systems, how fast would they have to travel to reach us?"

"Fast, but not as fast as the speed of light," Ed offered.

"Do you think the speed of light is the fastest speed, Ed?" I wanted to know.

"As far as we know," he answered.

"I wonder," I said.

"Are you questioning this?"

"No, but I was thinking of thoughts. Surely, our thoughts are faster than the speed of light. I can transfer myself in a split second to another planetary system, simply by my thoughts."

Ed chuckled. "But surely, you cannot compare your thoughts to light, can you?"

"No. On the other hand, I don't know what light consists of, just as I don't know what thoughts consist of. What I do know is, light and thoughts have different properties, and thoughts are faster than light."

"You don't mean to imply that UFOs may arrive

here by mere thoughts of some aliens, do you?" Gottlieb wanted to know.

I shrugged. "Perhaps some form of ESP transmission is possible," I said.

Gottlieb shook his head.

Ed gave me a squinting look, deep in thought. He no doubt evaluated this possibility.

We sat in silence again for quite some time.

"Well, enough speculation, I think I'll turn in," said Gottlieb. With that, he got up and disappeared into our tent. Ed and I finished our smokes, poured some water on our campfire, and then joined Gottlieb.

During the 1970s, Ed caught some kind of brain disease. He told me his doctor said it was a fungus, which beer could have caused. Ed ended up in a veterans' hospital in Edmonton, where I paid him frequent visits. I couldn't detect any loss of brainpower, though. Ed was as sharp as ever, but he now had a sad look in his eyes.

I felt like cheering him up: "You'll be better in no time, Ed, and we'll go fishing again."

I got no response from him and tried a different tack: "Do you remember, Ed, when we discussed Bertrand Russell's essay, *Why I Am Not A Christian*?"

"Yes."

"Do you believe there are some true benefits to be a Christian?"

"There would be if Christians could follow all the teachings of Jesus."

"You mean, such as when Jesus said, love not

only your neighbor but also your enemy?"

"That's not an exact quote, but, yes, that's what I mean."

"It's a very hard task, don't you agree?"

"It's an impossible task in our world. We'll always have to live with conflicts."

"Don't you think that love could conquer our conflicts?"

"This would go against the universal design."

I looked puzzled.

He continued to explain: "The universal design depends on pairs of opposites. Every north has a south, every east a west, every up has a down, good pairs with evil, there are males and females, we have black and white, positive needs negative, and so on, and love, to be recognized, requires hate. Take hate away, and love ceases to exist. I'm surprised Jesus didn't realize this, although He did speak also of heaven and hell."

"Perhaps Jesus genuinely believed that true love could conquer hate."

"Well, in any case, it doesn't change the universal design. We can throw things off balance sometimes, and human beings are famous for doing just that, but, in the end, we have to return to a balance. You cannot have only positives or negatives, or only females or males, or only black or white. These opposites are part of our universal design, and so is love and hate."

"You mean good also requires evil?"

"Yes. What would *good* be if you couldn't compare it to *evil*?"

When I didn't respond immediately, he smiled and said, "Let's take a look at the concept of 'right' and 'wrong.' Here you have a controversial subject that you could argue about for many years. What's 'right' in one country could well be 'wrong' in another. It all depends on what we were taught."

I shook my head. "But surely there must be some basics that we can all agree on, like, for instance, murder being wrong."

"Even murder is sanctioned by some societies. For example, some tribes in the jungle kill their elders to provide lacking meat for the community. Then, take our wars, or take capital punishment. These killings are nothing more than murder sanctioned by the state. In these cases, even Christian countries do not practice Jesus's command to love their enemies."

"You make a good point, Ed," I said as I got up and stretched myself. "Well, it's getting late. I must run along, Ed." I shook his hand: "See you soon, my friend."

I will forever cherish Ed's intellect – his logical observations and his sound advice. I had a few more conversations with him at the veterans' hospital, but it seemed to me that he was gradually losing interest in any deeper subjects, although he was always glad to see me. I still miss our truth-seeking discussions.

Lastly, his disease must have been much more serious than what he had led us to believe, because he passed away rather suddenly in September 1981, a month after his sixty-sixth birthday.

7

Gordon Hammond

Pete Raffin, Gordon Hammond, Walter Lawrence, and Renee.

I had casually met Gordon Hammond at various association meetings. We became better acquainted at the first convention of the Electrical Contractors Association of Alberta (ECAA) in 1967. Despite being keen competitors, we soon became good friends.

One day, he and I drove back to Edmonton from an ECAA board of directors' meeting in Calgary. We stopped in Red Deer to have some dinner. After dinner, as we were relaxing with our coffees, Gordon gave me a speculative look and said, "I hear you're claiming that apprentices can't save us any money."

Arthur O.R. Thormann

♣

I had joined Jake Matthews, another competitor, teaching an estimating course, and I told our students they should not assume that they could save money by employing apprentices.

"It's true," I said, "providing you give apprentices a proper training and don't use them merely for repetitive work."

"I'm still lost to see how they won't save us any money," he said.

"Let me give you a simplified example, Gordon. Suppose a contractor's journeyman-cost per hour comes to $20.00 and his apprentice-cost per hour comes to $10.00."

He interrupted me: "For a first-year apprentice?"

"Yes. Then, suppose a journeyman must train an apprentice for two hours to be able to install a certain piece of electrical equipment. The task normally takes one hour to complete, and, after the two-hour training session, the journeyman and the apprentice take the rest of the day, six hours, to each install six pieces of equipment."

Gordon nodded.

"So, by using the apprentice for the equipment installation, including the training cost the contractor's production cost is $60.00 for the installation time plus $60.00 for the training time – the training cost consists of $20.00 for the apprentice and $40.00 for the journeyman. This comes to a total of $120.00."

Gordon nodded in agreement.

I continued, "And, by using the journeyman for the equipment installation, the contractor's production cost is simply six times the journeyman's hourly cost, also $120.00. Therefore, the production costs using the apprentice and the journeyman are identical."

Gordon laughed. "You used an example that supports your theory, Art, but what about reality? Have you tried your theory in practice to find out if it works?"

"I've tried it out on a few small projects, Gordon. On these projects, I have used only journeymen, although my budgets consisted of a composition of journeymen and apprentices, using an average rate. However, even at the higher journeymen rate, my budgets were not exceeded, because my journeymen used fewer hours than the budget."

"Well, I'll be darned!" said Gordon. He sat there thinking. Then he asked, "What percentage of your budget hours did they use up?"

"Eighty percent, which, incidentally, is the same percentage I apply to the journeyman-cost per hour to come up with my composite average rate for journeymen and apprentices. To calculate the average rate, I use four journeymen, including a sub foreman, plus one first-, one second-, one third-, and one fourth-year apprentice."

"Yes, that's the common practice," said Gordon. He sat there thinking again. Then he laughed. "It might work on smaller projects," he admitted, "but larger projects have more repetitive work. I don't believe your theory would hold water on larger projects."

"Not on all of them, I must admit, and especially not if contractors use apprentices just as glorified laborers – to do the simple, repetitive work – and refuse to give them proper training."

Gordon nodded. "By the way, you've just received an electrical contract for a large project," he said, "the new Law Courts Building in Edmonton. Did you get started on it yet?"

"We've only done some preliminary planning, so far."

"Is there much repetitive work on this project?"

"There is some repetitive work, but it cannot be performed continuously: It's spread out over the two-and-a-half-year construction schedule."

"Therefore, according to your theory, you could do this job with journeymen only without exceeding your labor budget?"

"I could, I suppose."

"Would you?"

I hesitated.

"You're wavering, aren't you?"

"It's not because I think the theory won't work on this project. It's because I don't know if Vic Webb will back me. I have a quarter-million dollar labor budget on this project, you know." Vic Webb was the owner of Progress Electric, the company I managed.

"Well, just in case you decide to put your theory to a meaningful test, I'll make you a bet that you'll exceed your budget."

"What are you betting, Gordon?"

"A t-bone steak dinner and a bottle of your favorite wine," he smiled, not expecting me to bite.

"You're on."

♣

"What about Vic Webb?"

"I think I can convince him to go along with me. He's already convinced that apprentices don't save us any money in the end. He's a firm believer in giving apprentices their proper training, you know."

"All right, we have a bet, then?"

"Yes."

The Edmonton Law Courts Building actually took thirty-two months to complete. During the last two months, we finished another project that employed a few fourth-year apprentices I did not want to lose – lay off. I put a call through to Gordon: "Hello Gordon. I want to ask you something about our bet."

"What do you want to ask me?"

"I have some fourth-year apprentices I don't want to lay off. I can put them to work on the Law Courts Building. Would that cancel your bet?"

"How far are you completed?"

"I'd say, about ninety-seven percent."

"How much of your labor budget have you used up?'

"Ninety-seven percent."

"You're kidding. Have you used any apprentices on the job?"

"No."

"Then, I'd say you've already won the bet. Go ahead and put your fourth-year apprentices to work."

"Thanks, Gordon."

"Gosh, I can't believe you actually proceeded with your idea. I was just joking when I made you that bet, you know."

"Does that mean you're not going to buy me a t-bone-steak dinner?" I laughed.

"No, you'll get your dinner, all right, along with a bottle of wine. What you have proven is very valuable."

"Well, I had to prove the theory to you and to my students, but to myself as well. Also, Vic Webb is breathing easier now."

Gordon and I chose Hy's Steakhouse for dinner. Gordon ordered a filet mignon and I ordered a t-bone steak. The waiter enquired regarding the choice of wine. Gordon raised his eyebrows and looked at me.

"A Châteauneuf-du-Pape," I said.

"We have E. Guigal and La Crau," said the waiter.

"E. Guigal is fine," I said. Gordon smiled. He knew that E. Guigal was the less expensive of the two.

"I've agreed to convey an offer from Stan Sunley to you, Art."

Stan Sunley was one of our competitors: the owner of Sunley Electric. "What's his offer?" I wanted to know.

"He wants you to manage his business for him."

"He couldn't pay me enough to do that, Gordon."

"Oh, I don't know, he'll probably pay you more than Vic Webb."

"That's not enough," I smiled. "You know darn well that he would run interference. Vic Webb leaves the running of his business to me, period."

"Vic Webb is very fortunate to have someone like you, and Stan Sunley knows this. Stan is getting on in age, and his sons are not interested in running an electrical contracting business. You could probably take Stan's business over completely, eventually."

"The same applies to Vic Webb's business, and I like working for him."

"Well, think about it, Art."

"There's not much to think about, Gordon. I just don't trust old Stan that much – with my future, I mean."

Gordon shrugged. "I would make you an offer myself if I intended to stay in the business of electrical contracting."

This was news to me. "You intend to get out of electrical contracting?"

"Yes, I'm looking at some other options. Electrical contracting doesn't pay enough for my efforts and the risks I'm taking."

"The business can be quite profitable, Gordon, if one is able to find enough exceptional, competitive advantages."

"I know *you* do, Art, but I've never been creative enough to find any advantages. Honestly, I don't know how you do it. I keep hearing rumors all the time that your prices are too low and that you'll go broke, but here you are, alive and well. Pete Raffin was telling me, after you landed the Law Courts Building, that this would be the last straw – now you'll go broke for sure."

"We've made a good profit on the Law Courts

Building, Gordon."

"I don't know how you do it, Art."

"It's really simple, Gordon: My motto is this: If I can't buy it for the right price, I'll make it myself."

"I couldn't do that. I wouldn't know how to do that."

"I've been involved in manufacturing during my first apprenticeship, and what I've learned there gives me the courage to tackle anything that comes along – no matter how complex and how complicated, Gordon."

He gives me an admiring look and raises his wine glass: "Well, here's to success," he says.

We clink our glasses together and enjoy a sip of the expensive French wine. We sit in silence for a minute. Then Gordon says, "There couldn't have been much you might manufacture at the Law Courts Building."

He was now pushing me into territory that is more dangerous: To reveal to him some of my trade secrets. However, I didn't mind telling him what I did at the Law Courts Building. "That's not true, Gordon, there was quite a lot I could and did manufacture."

"Do you mind telling me what that was?"

"Not at all, my friend: For example, we manufactured all wall plates for the electrical devices – thousands of them, Gordon."

"But, surely, you could have bought these from various suppliers as well."

"Yes, but we couldn't buy these plates for the right price, Gordon. Remember my motto: If I can't

♣

buy it for the right price, I'll make it myself. Our suppliers wanted more than three times what it cost me to make these plates."

"Awesome!" said Gordon. "What was so special about these plates?"

"They had to have a special, architectural-bronze finish. We ordered large sheets of special brass alloy from a manufacturer in Winnipeg. Then, after cutting and shaping the plates, we had them polished, oxidized, and oil-rubbed to attain the specified finish. We were the first ones to get the architect's approval. The only snag was that the Winnipeg manufacturer required a minimum quantity of sheets for the production of the special alloy, and I had to face the situation and order them. However, that, too, ended up to be profitable, because few other trades could afford to order this minimum quantity of sheets. We ended up either supplying them the sheets or making their plates. We even made our fire alarm panel and annunciator covers."

"What about the tools for shaping the plates and cutting the special holes in the plates and covers"? Gordon wanted to know.

"I had these tools made by the Stamco Company to my specifications."

"Amazing!" said Gordon. "No wonder you make money on jobs at prices that would bankrupt other contractors."

"That's only part of it."

"You mean there's more?"

I nodded. "You must also know when the prices

are right or wrong, Gordon. I price out all special equipment in my estimates long before I get the suppliers' prices. Then, I enter my prices in a spreadsheet for comparison with the suppliers. I can even determine if the suppliers' lot prices, the prices that contain various lots of materials and equipment, are too high by comparing them to my estimate."

"I've never been able to do that," said Gordon. "I wouldn't even know where to begin."

"It's not too hard if you know something about manufacturing. Manufacturing a piece of equipment is no different than installing materials on the job: You have to break down the piece of equipment into its component parts; then, price out these parts and add up the prices to get the total cost of the piece of equipment."

Gordon nodded. "And you're wondering why I want to get out of the electrical business. I can see now how you make your profits, but I couldn't do it, Art. I'm competing with low competitors without knowing what to do to lower my costs. I can also see why Stan wants to hire you."

During the early 1970s, Gordon and I were also involved in the drafting of the first set of trade definitions in Alberta for the electrical trade. The task turned out to be controversial, especially with the mechanical trade. The mechanical trade had historically supplied electrical motors, usually as a part of mechanical equipment. Furthermore, the mechanical trade had frequently also supplied the electrical controls for these motors – both operational and protective controls – and the electrical trade raised an objection to the mechanical trade supplying these controls. Thus, our task was not only to draft these trade definitions but also to negotiate with the mechanical trade regarding their content.

My approach was simple: Since the electrical trade was connecting these controls, and often installing them too, the electrical trade should also supply them. This seemed black-and-white logic to me. However, the mechanical trade disagreed with this logic and included these controls in its trade definitions. Gordon Hammond arranged a meeting with the mechanical trade and asked Gordon Alexander, the manager of the Alberta Construction Association, to chair it. Before the meeting, Gordon Hammond and I had a quick lunch to discuss our strategy.

"How do you propose to sell them on the idea to let us supply the motor controls?" Gordon asked me.

"It's a logical conclusion, Gordon."

"I know, but they use a different logic."

"Their logic is wrong."

"They claim that the controls run their equipment and, therefore, are part of their equipment."

"On the other hand, some of these controls perform protective functions, and the electrical trade is trained to make a proper determination for them."

"That's a good point, Art. Still, the mechanical boys will give us counter arguments. So, can we propose a compromise solution to them?"

"I hate to compromise on an issue of such

importance, Gordon."

"I know, but if we find some middle ground, Gordon Alexander will side with us. If we're obstinate about this issue, he'll side with the mechanical boys."

We sat in silence for a while. "Okay," I said, "how about this? Let's propose to them that they can supply all controls that have mechanical and electrical connections, and we shall supply all controls that have only electrical connections."

"That is probably the fairest solution I've heard so far, and I'm sure Gordon Alexander would support this proposal."

"Let's propose it, then, this afternoon," I said.

We did propose it and still got a few arguments from the mechanical boys, but Gordon Alexander was fed up with their arguments and told them plainly that this proposal was the best they could expect to get, with the support of the construction industry.

Gordon Hammond called me at the office one afternoon: "Can I buy you a pizza tonight, Art?"

"What's up?"

"I just want to buy you a pizza at my new pizza parlor."

"You're kidding! Where and what time do I join you?"

"Come to the Boston Pizza Restaurant on 118th Avenue at six o'clock."

At dinner that evening, Gordon told me he had sold his electrical contracting business and bought a Boston Pizza franchise. He said he regretted getting out of the contracting business but was looking forward to making some real money for a change.

"How much did you have to pay for the franchise?" I wanted to know.

"$250,000.00."

"That's a lot of money."

"It's worth it, Art. You have to measure the investment by the return, and the return is ten times what it is in the contracting business."

"Wow!"

He smiled and nodded.

I still kept consulting Gordon on various issues concerning the contracting business, usually over lunch or dinner at his pizza parlor, but I was aware that his interest in contracting was waning. He was more interested to let me know how much money he was making in his restaurant. At one point, he considered investing his excess money in a general contracting business and asked me if I want to run it for him. I declined, and he bought another Boston Pizza franchise.

One day, as we were sharing one of his pizzas, I noticed a swelling of his eyelids. I asked him what had caused this problem. He said he didn't know and was going to see a doctor about it. The doctor diagnosed him with cancer. "They've caught it early, though," he assured me, "and are confident that it can be cured."

In the next few months, Gordon got back to normal and said the cancer was in remission. Then, it suddenly started up again. Renee, his wife, tried desperately to save him with large doses of vitamins and minerals, to no avail in the end. I regularly paid him visits in the W.W. Cross Hospital. On the last day I saw him alive, I noticed a big swelling in his abdomen. He didn't look well and was just receiving chemotherapy. I asked him how he was feeling.

"Fine," he said. "Once they get rid of this thing," pointing to his abdomen, "I'm out of here."

"I wish there were something I can do, Gordon."

"I know, Art, I know."

I had tears in my eyes as I drove home that day, and the following lines flashed through my mind: "A friend who is dying can render your heart as sore as the flesh that is pierced by a dart; for once you are tongue-tied and no longer smart: You feel helpless. Your heart is a throbbing and tenderized sore; you want to reach out and touch him once more. But the distance' too great and the silence' a roar: You are strengthless."

One week after this last visit, Gordon died at a relatively young age of 53. To this day, I still remember our good times and our constructive discussions together.

8

Carl Leviston

Carl Leviston, leaning back in smug comfort.

Carleton (Carl) Wilson Leviston was our company lawyer. Vic Webb, my boss, first introduced me to him. Vic assured me that Carl was a good lawyer. He assured me that Carl had once been, after all, a law professor at some university in Ontario. That had impressed me, of course.

I was even more impressed with Carl the more I became acquainted with him. Whenever Vic and I went to his office for advice, perhaps ready to sue someone, Carl played the devil's advocate, eventually talking us out of our complaint. A prominent little sign on his desk read, "Are you sure it's justice you want?" This summed up Carl's attitude perfectly – probably in response to some of his clients' demands. Many clients want things their way, naturally, but their way may not be the way of justice.

At first, Carl's opposing viewpoint annoyed me, and I mentioned this to Vic. He just laughed and said, "You can find many lawyers who would try to make a winning case of your complaint, only to find out eventually that you're the loser – both legally and financially. Carl is trying to prevent that." Ultimately, I realized that Vic was right.

Carl was as good a carpenter as he was a lawyer. He built boats and even built his own house. I had to drive to Carl's house, occasionally, to deliver, or to pick up some documents. He usually offered me an alcoholic drink of some kind. I, in turn, admired his latest home-built boat and his Mexican souvenirs. He also told me various stories about his backwoods' travels in Mexico, and we seldom spent less than two hours together, eventually exchanging fishing experiences. Carl had one of his boats moored in the Fraser River at Vancouver. He took it out deep-sea fishing occasionally and invited me to come along, but I could never find the time.

I never found out how Carl made his living. I knew that he owned some commercial properties, and I wondered many times if these properties provided him with a sufficient income. As for his legal fees, I was sure they did not even pay for the overhead of his legal practice. I even had to remind him occasionally, mostly at year-ends, to send us an invoice for his services. Sometimes he would just tell me to send him a check for whatever I thought his services were worth to us. Perhaps he was afraid he might overcharge us.

Carl took a couple of months out of each winter to travel to Mexico for a vacation. He arranged with another lawyer to look after his clients during this time. The other lawyer worked pretty well with the same philosophy as Carl did, and we never experienced any disappointments with him, but we were still glad when Carl returned and took over again.

Carl's main value to me was his willingness to teach me something about the law, and I proved to be an attentive apprentice. I remember one time when we had to prepare for discoveries. I wanted some instructions on how I should respond to questions by the opposing lawyer. Carl said, "The usual response is very short and direct. Most lawyers will instruct you not to volunteer any information – especially no information that could give you an advantage at trial."

"Is that what you want me to do, Carl?"

"Well, this is not always the wisest course of action, unless you're hell-bent to go to trial."

"Can you be more explicit?"

"Well, yes. I prefer to let the other party know what my strong suit is. That way, I may get a settlement offer and save the cost of a trial."

"You mean, I should volunteer information about the strength of our case if I have the chance?"

"That might be the wisest course of action."

I kept this in mind during the following

discoveries, but the opposing lawyer never gave me an opportunity to volunteer any information damaging to his client's case. Finally, I asked him if I could say something off the record. He nodded and Carl agreed as well. I freely told this lawyer what could damage his client's case. His client was listening carefully to everything I said. Then his client requested a recess. Both of them left the room. The opposing lawyer returned after a few minutes and asked Carl to join him for a brief conference. He gave Carl a settlement offer. Carl came back into the room and conferred with me. We decided that the offer was good enough without making a counteroffer, and Carl conveyed our acceptance.

With the discoveries concluded, Carl and I went for lunch and discussed the matter. I was glad that I did not have to spend any more time on this case, and I thanked Carl for his sound advice. Carl smiled and said, "Many court cases could simply be settled in a similar fashion if the parties were more trusting and less insistent upon a trial."

That was Carl's way. He did not believe in the infallibility of judges. "Judges are human like the rest of us," he would assert, "and they make mistakes like the rest of us."

On the other hand, Carl was also stubborn, especially when dealing with other lawyers. When he knew he was right, he would hang onto his position until the other lawyer gave up, perhaps out of sheer frustration. I remember when John Skolimoski, my mother's third husband, died, and his son hired a lawyer to get more of the estate than Carl figured he should get. Carl explained my mother's position to the stepson's lawyer and then, stubbornly, stuck to it. He eventually got the settlement he wanted, and my mother was very happy with the outcome.

I received most of my legal education and advice from Carl over lunch. Carl liked cheap buffet lunches, usually with the food piled high on his plate. I was more conservative. The topics we covered varied substantially during our many lunches together – some of them were hypothetical in nature. As an example, I asked him one day what to do about customers who are slow payers or who don't pay us at all.

"If a customer doesn't pay you for services rendered, is that considered unjust enrichment, Carl?"

"It's possible. In your line of business, I would assume that you provided the service, probably at the request of the customer, and that the service was of some value to the customer and should be paid for." I nodded, and Carl continued: "So, the question I must ask is: Why doesn't the customer pay for the service? Usually, I'm led to investigate whether the customer is dissatisfied with the service, or whether no payment arrangements were made, or whether the customer is short of funds."

"But doesn't this still amount to unjust enrichment?"

"Yes, but you'd be well advised to investigate the reasons for nonpayment before taking any legal actions."

I thought about his advice for a few seconds and

then asked him, "I gave a friend of mine a loan, Carl, and he's not repaying it, even after a few gentle hints from me. Isn't that considered unjust enrichment?"

"Did you make any arrangements for the repayment of the loan?"

"No. I just took for granted that he would repay the loan within a reasonable time."

"Then there's no due date for the repayment?"

"No."

"So, if you took your friend to court, he could simply tell the judge that he'll repay the loan whenever he's able to do so. That wouldn't constitute unjust enrichment. However, the judge may tie your friend to a more definite repayment schedule, but you would still have to wait. Unjust enrichment would only apply if your friend were unwilling to repay the loan."

"Thanks for the advice, Carl. We're probably too lax in our dealings with customers as well. Perhaps we should agree up front with them when payments for services rendered are due."

Carl nodded and added, "As I recall, the contracts with your general contractors are the best examples of being lax on your part: In most cases, these contracts state that you'll get paid when the general contractor gets paid. Therefore, no payment is due until then. And, if the general contractor never gets paid, no payment is ever due!" He gave me one of his mocking see-what-I-mean?-serves-you-right smiles. "You can't even claim unjust enrichment, Art, because you've agreed to these unfair terms."

On another day, over lunch again, we discussed

one of my construction delay claims. "Make sure you avoid double-dipping," Carl advised. "Judges don't take kindly to it."

"Can you give me some examples?"

"Don't charge extra amounts for tools and supervision that you have already included in your labor charge-out rates."

"I'll keep that in mind. For a minute, I thought you might exclude either profit or interest charges."

"No. Profit and interest charges are both acceptable to the courts."

"That surprises me, Carl."

"Why should it? Judges, too, appreciate that businesses must make a profit to survive. And bank interest on overdrafts and loans is certainly a chargeable expense."

"I was thinking more of the profit as a return on investment rather than the profit as a risk premium, Carl. I believe that the profit charges as a return on investment and the bank interest charges are mutually exclusive."

"How do you come to that conclusion?"

"Consider from where the working capital of a business comes, Carl. It comes either from the shareholders or from the banks. If it comes completely from the shareholders, a profit must be charged by the business to pay dividends to the shareholders, and if it comes completely from the banks, interest must be charged by the business to satisfy the banks."

"But even if the banks put up all of the working capital, the shareholders will still demand a profit."

"The question is: Are the shareholders entitled to a profit if they have not put up any money?"

"The courts would allow it."

"Why? I thought the courts are averse to double-dipping."

"If a business can prove to the court that it had a legitimate interest expense, Art, the court would not relate that expense to a profit it thinks the business is entitled to earn."

"I would have been under the impression that the profit entitlement is at least partially cancelled by the interest-expense entitlement."

"I'm not aware of any court rulings to that effect."

"I find that strange."

Carl just shrugged. He was probably trying to tell me to leave well enough alone.

Carl also did some legal work for our families. He drafted our wills, took on some petty disputes, and, unreservedly, gave us advice. As mentioned previously, Carl also helped my mother settle the estate after her husband died and her stepson wanted to take over the farm.

When my mother asked me to help her with a farm lease, I turned again to Carl for assistance. Carl told me that the lease forms sold at office-supply stores are comprehensive and require few additions.

"Anything special I should observe when completing one of these forms, Carl?"

"The three things to observe are, the work the lessee is allowed and expected to perform on the land, the buildings and the fences, the amount the lessee is expected to pay and when payment is due, and the term of the lease."

"That's pretty basic, Carl. Can you give me some specifics to include?"

"Well, you might want to include a building and fence maintenance provision. Also, I usually include a percentage of the land that should be kept in summer-fallow – on a rotational basis."

I made a note of these suggestions. "Is there anything else?"

"Some landlords like to specify fertilizer requirements."

"I'm not conversant enough with fertilizers to be specific about the requirements, Carl."

"Neither am I. Generally speaking, the lessee should leave the land, buildings, and fences in no worse condition than they were when he took over. This is where the use of fertilizer may come in, and the agreement should stipulate this."

Ultimately, my efforts to familiarize myself with farm leases (and Carl's advice) turned out to be in vain. My mother proceeded without Carl and me.

However, the lessee she had chosen eventually tried, and partially succeeded, to cheat her out of the last year's lease payment. She begged Carl to help her. Carl wrote a letter of demand to the lessee, without effect. Then, he filed a Civil Claim with the Provincial Court of Alberta. Eventually, he negotiated a settlement with the lessee's legal counsel. My mother had to settle for less than two-thirds of what was owing to her (to avoid more expensive litigation) mainly because she did not enter into a proper lease agreement with the lessee.

Carl was always happy and ready to help the underdog, and I do not know to this day if my mother compensated him properly for his services.

In the early 1990s, Carl contracted cancer. After he had received his treatments, we continued our luncheon meetings, and I can vouch for it that the disease did not affect Carl's appetite. Nevertheless, his days were numbered. He died on July 25, 1995, at age 74. I sorely missed our ongoing discussions.

9

Floyd Brackett

*At an electrical contractors' convention in Jasper, Alberta, 1977.
Foreground left: Floyd Brackett.*

Floyd Brackett was a salesman and a co-owner of
Electrical Wholesalers Edmonton Ltd. He called on me
regularly to get orders for electrical materials.
However, Floyd and I also enjoyed a more personal
relationship. We met occasionally after work to have a
drink together. At such times, we exchanged views on
our problems of the day. Floyd was a very emotional
man, which was most evident when he played the
piano. It was quite natural for us to discuss spiritual
issues as well. He was a devout Catholic, but he didn't

mind voicing the occasional criticism of his religion. One day, he gave me two little brochures with such criticism. He was obviously uneasy about this and asked me to return them to him as soon as possible.

A few times, during our meetings, I gave him a copy of my latest poem and asked him to read it and comment on it. He usually admired the deeper meaning of the poem, but not without receiving additional explanations from me. One day, after we had thoroughly discussed the various implications of what he had just read, he asked me how I got started on writing poems.

"Well, Floyd, that's quite a story. I wrote my first poem around Christmas 1971. Just prior to Christmas, I was supervising a high-voltage-cable test in an underground manhole. Two electricians were performing the test, which involved disconnecting and reconnecting the high-voltage lines under power. At the time, we were unaware of a small amount of ground gas that was present in the manhole, which polluted the air, and during one of the disconnecting procedures, a small spark caused the polluted air to explode all around us. We were literally in the middle of a fiery cloud. The heat singed our hair, including our eyebrows and eyelashes. I was wearing an alpaca coat, and its hair had curled up into tiny brown balls. Worst of all, the white flash had blinded me. Coworkers who were outside the manhole rushed us to the nearest hospital. Thankfully, none of us was seriously hurt. The doctor told me that my blindness is temporary, similar to the experience of looking into a welding flash without proper goggles.

"So, I spent the next two weeks, including the holidays, in blindness. This gave me lots of time to think without the distraction of looking at my surroundings. During one of those days, a poem came to me in the German language, which I called *Die Suche nach dem Sinn des Lebens*. This title roughly translates to *The Search for Life's Meaning*. I say 'roughly' because I believe that the import of the German word *Sinn* includes both the English words 'meaning' and 'purpose'. The poem was rather long – seventy-two lines – and, because I couldn't see, I asked my wife, Renate, to write it down for me. She did, and I never changed a word in it since then. I liked the poem very much and always felt it should be translated into English, but, after some feeble attempts, I finally gave up on it."

I opened my briefcase, took out a copy of the original German version, and showed it to Floyd.

"Why don't you give me a rough idea of what it says, Art?"

"Okay, I'll try." Thus, I spent the remainder of the evening with Floyd in another feeble translation attempt.

Many years after Floyd died of cancer, at the relatively young age of sixty-one, I decided to try my translation attempts again. One of the reasons why my previous attempts failed was because I tried to be too literal. This not only lost the poem's rhyme, but it also proved to be impossible, in many cases, to find appropriate

English words. This time, I decided against any literal translation. I just wrote a similar poem in English – restating the original instead of translating it. Neither of the poem versions was ever published. I am including the restated poem in this chapter as a tribute to my good friend Floyd Brackett, whom I miss dearly.

The Search for Life's Meaning

If you ever wondered about life's delusion,
Even when you're getting close to your conclusion,
If you wanted to know what it was all about,
Or why you went along your chosen route,
And no answers met you readily: do not dismay;
Keep searching, since you seek a needle in the hay.

During your search, you're blinded first by wealth;
To get it, you must fight despite your harm to health;
Yet, this kind of competition story
Never ends up in a worthwhile glory.
You're unhappy, too: all expectation's lost,
Because it never buys you what is needed most.

Now your search meets up with awe-inspiring power,
You bid it "Hail!" and soon adore it like a flower;
To dominate your fellows around you
Is what excites, and what is stimulating, too.
But you make enemies, who hate you, by the score,
And, finally, you're the one who loses out galore.

Next you believe with presents to obtain
That which your heart was unable to gain;
But here, too, your search meets no satisfaction,

106

Floyd Brackett

♣

Since most folks expect very different action:
What's fair to one is not another's ticket,
You're good this once and then again just wicked.

Suddenly, you look at all your troubles anew,
As if they were consciously aimed at you;
And to escape the ridicule of the rude,
You seek some bliss in inner solitude;
You feel even lost amidst all the fashion –
It seems like you've also lost your passion.

Meeting those who claim to have found,
And others who in darkness abound:
The fools, the meek, the happy, and the ailing,
Make you even more aware of your failing:
"Who's right?" – is what your problem is –
"Who has the belief that cannot miss?"

At last you meet up with scholarly men;
In belief to have found, you're adoring them;
The new wisdom causes your eyes to open:
It seems your new life is all set and coping.
But soon it is clear: the new wisdom is crumbling,
And new search's haste is ending in fumbling.

Your searching trip denies you convalescence,
And, in your plight, you turn to higher essence:
You hope through prolonged prayers to attempt
That your deeds will not be forever condemned.
But doubt ensues you with an inner mock,
And your words are as barren as seeds on a rock.

If you can count yourself among the lucky ones
Who can still choose after their striving runs,
You may come up with the brilliant conception

Arthur O.R. Thormann

♣

That all things in your thought collection
Add up to only two good conditions,
Together with a meaningful mission:

You must live your life lacking futile fear,
To eliminate useless worries here;
Since plenty of worries come easy enough,
Best save them for those times that are rough.
Your courage is needed to face certainty,
And to avoid some deceptions of reality.

With compassion you must spend your day,
To help those you meet along your way;
And with patience, not with undue haste,
You must seek to serve, with genuine grace;
And your deeds should include the kind of love
That is also required to keep you above.

Then, finally, you must give all back,
Which fell into your hands along the trek:
Your possessions, your mind, and even your heart,
To give human beings a better start.
This action will be your contribution
To the cycle of life and its evolution.

Restated in English: December 2008
(German version: December 1971)

108

10

Paul Black

On June 4, 2008, I received an email from Gregory Black informing me of his father Paul's grave illness; he suggested that I call his mother for more details. I put a call through to Joyce, Paul's wife, and she said, "Hold on, I'll let you speak to Paul." It took a minute for her to get Paul on the line, and when he greeted me, I was shocked at his slurry speech. He was obviously laboring to say a few words to me, but I could hardly understand what he was trying to tell me, especially about the nature of his illness. He did manage to convey to me that he could hardly swallow, but that it did not affect his mind. He also said that the disease is probably incurable. I told him to hang in there and asked him to let me speak to Joyce. He called out for her to take the phone. I told Joyce that I couldn't understand Paul's description of the disease. She said, "He has a lower motor neuron disease. Thankfully, it's not the upper motor neuron disease, which is usually fatal." Then she described some of the differences to me. I knew, of course, that, with her background as a nurse, she would have done a thorough research on the disease. I told her that Renate (my wife) and I were heading out to Vancouver shortly, but I would phone again after our return to find out if Paul had made any progress.

We returned from Vancouver on June 15, Father's Day, and late that afternoon I received a phone call from Gregory to tell me that his father had died at 4:20 p.m. that afternoon. I was shocked, of course. All I could mutter was, "Oh, that's so sad." He promised to keep me informed about the funeral arrangements.

I phoned Harold Taylor, a fellow trustee, to give him the sad news. He said that, if I felt up to it, I should attend the funeral to represent the trustees, since Paul, as our first investment manager, had done a lot to increase the assets of our fund.

The next few days were hectic. I phoned Gregory on Monday to get the arrangements for the funeral. He said they scheduled it for Friday at 11:00 a.m., at Our Lady of Sorrows Church in Toronto. Then, I arranged to send flowers to the church and a sympathy card to Joyce on behalf of the trustees. Next, I searched the internet for reasonably priced flights. Most flights were outrageously expensive, and I did not want to fly at 1:00 a.m. on Friday morning to save a few dollars. I did a similar search for downtown Toronto hotels for Thursday night. Adding up the cost to attend Paul's funeral almost made me change my mind.

Usually, we base our actions for a particular cause on the three Cs of care, cost, and convenience. If we care enough about the cause, cost and inconvenience become non-issues, providing we can afford it, of course; otherwise, cost and inconvenience become major issues. Once I had decided that I cared enough to join Paul's family at the funeral, I stopped thinking about cost and inconvenience and started to make my travel arrangements.

I flew out of Edmonton at 5:00 p.m. on Thursday

and arrived in Toronto at 10:45 p.m., just in time to catch the 10:55 p.m. Airport Express Bus to take me downtown, where I checked into the Fairmont Royal York Hotel. Then I phoned Renate, to let her know that I had arrived safely, and went to the Union Station to buy some subway tickets. I finally went to bed well past midnight.

After a sound sleep, I got up at six, shaved, packed my bag, checked out, handed my bag to the bellman for storage, ate a brief breakfast of oatmeal and yoghurt, had a meeting with Rick Brooks-Hill, our second investment manager, and caught the subway train to the Royal York Station, the closest station to the church.

I arrived at the church a half hour early, which gave me a chance to greet Joyce and her children Gregory, John, Paul Jr., Stephanie, and Catherine outside. Joyce was happy to see me, and Gregory thanked me for coming. Just before we went inside, Joyce pointed sadly to the hearse and said, "There's Paul; all we can do now is pray for him."

The funeral proceedings followed a typical Roman Catholic ceremony. I had a good view from the third pew on the left and watched Joyce, who was sitting in the first seat of the first pew on the right. Although, I am sure, she felt distressed, she held up extremely well. I had the impression that the words uttered by the priest neither increased nor decreased her sorrow.

After the ceremony, we gathered outside in front of the church again, getting ready for the funeral procession to the Mount Pleasant Cemetery. I suggested to Gregory that I would meet them for the reception at the Royal Canadian Military Institute, since I didn't have a car to join the procession. At first, Gregory proposed that I should take a taxi: "It's not that far," he said, but when I declined, he quickly arranged a ride for me with Peter and Jean Whyte. Peter worked with Paul many years ago, and readily agreed to take me along. Peter's car was the last one in the procession. We must have taken quite a detour – with a police escort along freeways and around the far side of Mount Pleasant – because it took us almost forty-five minutes to enter the cemetery grounds. Peter found a place to park the car, and we just arrived in time to hear a junior priest say a few more words of final assurance. Six military men and a bagpiper also honored the internment. Just before the pallbearers lowered the casket into the ground, each close family member put a rose on it. Some other family members and friends each took a flower from one of the delivered arrangements and put it on the casket. Then, Joyce gave the casket one last farewell kiss, and most of the attendants headed back to their cars.

I was walking back slowly beside Peter, who was limping along with a cane because of an earlier injury to his foot, which didn't affect his driving ability, however. On the way to the Royal Canadian Military Institute to attend the reception, Peter told me that the priest at the church, with all his gestures and loud voice, reminded him of Mussolini. When we arrived at the institute, the Blacks' guests already well attended the place. For some reason, I felt hungry. Normally, I do not eat or drink much at funerals. It always amazes me how hungry people can get on such occasions. This reception was no different. The servers steadily brought out new sandwiches and hors d'oeuvres, and the beer, wine, and alcohol flowed freely. In the packed room, I managed to get close enough to Joyce to say a few more words of comfort to her. She received my sympathies graciously but didn't seem in need of them at that moment, with all the attention she was getting from various well-wishers. I did not stay long; I said my good-byes to the closest family members and took the subway back to the hotel to pick up my bag and head back to Edmonton.

Paul and I are relaxing on a chesterfield in his living room. He is unusually serious on this occasion.

I first met Paul Black Sr. in June 1973, when he was

still the president of Charterhouse Investment Management Limited. Paul, upon the recommendation of our consultant, John Sparling, applied to the Electrical Industry Pension Trust Fund of Alberta to manage its assets. I was one of four trustees of the trust fund who interviewed him. We were very impressed with his bond-trading record, and we saw no problem in hiring him and his company. In later years, we also decided to stay with Paul whenever he changed to or started new companies, like Black, Galper & Heessels, Ltd., for example.

Paul was an ardent bond trader – the best. He watched the spreads like a hawk and took full advantage of them. Even in a bearish year, he could outperform the average investment manager. He tried to explain his methods to me, but the normal investor, including me, would have neither the time nor the resources to take full advantage of this knowledge. If one could take full advantage of this knowledge, the benefits would be enormous. For one thing, the return on one's investment is very satisfactory and, for another thing, the risk of capital loss is minimal.

Paul was not only a knowledgeable and capable investment manager, but he also had presence and charisma – and he certainly liked entertaining his friends. The parties he threw were always lavish. To assure the satisfaction of his guests, he did not spare any expenses. Paul often held these parties in conjunction with investment conferences, which take place at various cities and resorts. This gave him many opportunities to alter his social programs. Sometimes, he would even charter a bus or a boat to take his guests sightseeing or deep-sea fishing.

Paul was a very polite person. I remember one occasion after we had attended a conference welcome reception at the Southampton Princess Hotel in Bermuda. Paul had invited me to join him, John Sparling, and their wives, Joyce and Mary, for dinner at the Henry VIII Restaurant. I was alone at the convention and had no other plans for the evening, so I accepted his invitation. John Sparling seemed to be in a foul mood. He had obviously had too many drinks at the reception. We no sooner sat down at the Henry VIII, and he started complaining about a person who had offended him at the reception. He also used obscene language to describe the person. Normally, I would not have been embarrassed, but we were in the company of ladies, and I did not appreciate this sort of misbehavior. John dominated the conversation and kept effing his way all through dinner. The women, embarrassed, I'm sure, decided the men were busy with shoptalk and engaged in their own conversation. John tried to get Paul and me to agree with him. Paul just nodded occasionally. He was too polite to shut up one of his guests. I just ignored John, which made him even more irate and obscene. At the end of the evening, I had lost what little respect I'd had for John. I've spent a few disagreeable evenings in my life, but this one takes the prize. Paul knew, of course, how I felt, and he apologized later for John's misbehavior.

Paul preferred fancy, expensive restaurants, serving mainly Western foods. I remember one time when we were attending an investment conference in Waikiki. Paul and Joyce had invited Renate and me to join them for lunch at the Ala Moana Hotel. The hotel had several restaurant choices, and Paul and Joyce were debating which one to pick. Renate and I enquired if they would like to go to one of our favorites, a little Korean restaurant, just a few blocks from their hotel. They reluctantly agreed – as a favor to us, I think. Paul wanted to order a taxi, but I talked him out of it: "The walk will do you good, Paul." However, neither Paul nor Joyce were used to walking outside too far, especially in eighty-plus-degree temperatures, and were sweating even after a relatively short stroll.

The restaurant was not too appealing either – no more than a hole in the wall – but having already agreed to join us, Paul and Joyce couldn't very well back out at this point. The menu was something else. Paul and Joyce looked at it with obvious alarm. I smiled and offered to do the ordering for all of us, and they gladly accepted. The server served us first some Korean condiment-type appetizers, without an order from us. Both Paul and Joyce seemed to like these small portions, judging by their appetites. For the main dishes, I had ordered some of our favorites: Japchae, Goonmandu, Bibimbap, Bulgogi, and Bulgalbi, and I was pleased to watch Paul and Joyce devour these dishes. Both were commenting on the delightful food at very reasonable prices.

Of course, we drank only water and green tea. This restaurant served no alcoholic beverages. Therefore, after we finished our lunch, Renate and I suggested the Willows Restaurant for a relaxing afternoon over Hawaiian cocktails. Paul and Joyce readily agreed with us. The restaurant is located in what looks like any ordinary city street and, when we arrived inside, both were surprised at the jungle-like setting of it.

Relaxing with our cocktails, they were still complimenting us on our excellent lunch suggestion. Neither of them had enjoyed Korean food before. Joyce said that it surely pays to be adventurous sometimes.

Paul, my wife, Renate, and I, inside the Willows Restaurant.

Talking about being adventurous, Paul loved to take his guests on boat cruises. Whether deep-sea fishing off the Bermuda Islands, or an Ottawa River leisure cruise from Hull to the Chateau Montebello, or a harbor cruise in the San Diego Bay to inspect the US

Naval Fleet, or a historic sightseeing cruise down the St. Lawrence River, Paul loved them all. I remember the latter one very well.

One time in May, after attending a government-legislation-update conference in Ottawa, we drove to Kingston, Ontario, where we checked into a local hotel. On the first day, Paul, who also had colonel status (in the Canadian Civil Defense division, I believe) first led us to the Fort Henry National Historic Site and then to the Royal Military College, where we were treated to a lunch in the mess hall and afterwards shown the college facilities.

For the following day, Paul had chartered a boat to take us down the St. Lawrence River. The plan was to go on an historic sightseeing cruise past Howe Island and various other islands and then head back along the opposite bank of the river to have a dinner at a restaurant on Wolfe Island, and finally return to Kingston.

It turned out to be an extremely interesting cruise. On the way back, darkness descended on us before we reached Wolfe Island, but the captain assured us that he did not have a problem finding his way. As it happened, he did have a problem, and we became a little anxious watching his groping attempts to reach Wolfe Island. Finally, he docked the boat, much later than Paul had scheduled, and Paul dismissed him with an assurance that we would catch the last ferry to Kingston. Nevertheless, we enjoyed an excellent if late dinner together, as well as Paul's astute narrative of the military history of the island.

Paul Black

♣

Boat cruises were not the only excursions Paul loved; he also arranged overland tours for his friends. I still remember our adventurous wine-tasting tour through California's Napa Valley, and another wine-tasting tour that took us from Halifax over the Confederation Bridge to Prince Edward Island, where you would least expect to find vineyards. Then, there was the antique-hunting tour along the road from Hull to Montreal, where Joyce found all kinds of treasures. Paul and Greg also invited us to join them on a skiing trip that took us from Calgary to Lake Louis. However, only Greg joined the skiers. Paul practiced his skating on a frozen surface in front of the Chateau Lake Louis. All these trips were memorable and full of fun.

No doubt, Paul was fun loving, but I also remember his torment on one sad occasion: during the dying days of his son Raymund. We were all in San Francisco, and Paul and Joyce had decided to bring Raymund along. Raymund was suffering from some form of cancer, and the doctors had suspected the disease to be terminal. Paul, always the obligatory host, had invited a few friends for a late dinner. Renate and I had a previous commitment and excused ourselves, and Joyce had decided to stay in their suite and look after Raymund. During dinner, Paul took offence at something the waiter did or said and just walked out, leaving the bill to be paid by one of his guests. Later, when this guest complained to me about it, I explained to him what Paul's mental condition must have been at that time, with a dying son in his suite. The guest felt embarrassed and said he'd had

♣

absolutely no idea. Paul, who was always a gentleman and an attentive host, had been pushed past his limit on that day. Few of us can imagine the extreme anguish and stress under which he must have suffered.

As a hobby, Paul liked to collect antique guns. One day when I was vacationing in Victoria, BC, I ran across some rust-pitted, galleon cannons at Capital Iron[6] that the company had salvaged from the many shipwrecks off the shores of Vancouver Island. I had a brief notion to send one of these to Paul, more for fun than any other motive, but I soon dismissed the idea as being too expensive as an amusement. Depending on their condition, the cannons were expensive enough, but I also wanted an original hardwood cannon mount, and Capital Iron had only two of these in stock, both decrepit-looking but necessary accessories. I asked the department manager how much it would cost to ship one of the cannons and mounts to Toronto. He wanted to know where in Toronto, and I told him one of the residential districts. He scratched his head and said, "Well, the cannon weighs over a thousand pounds, and the mount weighs over two-hundred pounds; then, we'll also have to crate them, and if the shipment is not picked up at the depot, there'll be another delivery charge to the residence. I think you're looking at a minimum of $800.00 for shipping and handling." I nodded, thanked him, and forgot about the notion.

At another time, I mentioned to Paul that I had an antique flintlock pistol, dating back over two-hundred years. I asked him if he knew anyone who could assess

---

[6] Capital Iron is a renowned hardware store in Victoria.

the value of it. He said, "Sure. Ship it to me and I'll have a friend of mine take a look at it."

I had picked up this pistol at the Fife and Drum Antiques store in Lunenburg, NS, during one of my travels. It was a "Tower" model, with the original Crown and GR[7] stamped on the lock-plate. The manager of the store had told me he had had it appraised by a gun expert, and the expert verified for him that the make of the pistol dated back to 1775. The Canadian Military in Halifax had issued the pistol in 1804 with the issue number 155. The manager assured me that the pistol, even with a slightly pitted barrel, is in mint condition. I fell in love with it, and after some haggling – the manager wanted $1,200.00 for this "fine antique" – I settled to purchase it for $1,000.00 including the crating, insuring and shipping costs.

So, at Paul's invitation then, I dispatched the pistol off to him and waited for his call. Actually, I had contemplated making him a present of it, but I wanted first to determine its true value. The call came a few weeks later. Paul said, "I'm sorry, but my friend tells me that this pistol is a replica." I was stunned for a second and then said, "I don't believe it, Paul. It certainly looks original to me." Paul chuckled: "They can make replicas look very original, all right." I tried to think of something else. "Does your friend believe that the pistol can be fired?" I asked him. "Oh yes," said Paul. "It's made well enough to be fired."

"Okay," I said, "you might as well ship it back to me."

---

[7] GR is a commemoration to the reign of King Gorge I.

"Sorry about that, Art, but I believe my friend's opinion is very reliable."

After I hung up, I thought some more about this new development. Did the antique store manager dupe me? I didn't think so. Next, I searched the internet. There were two types of replica guns available. One type was made of cast zinc; even the screw heads were part of the cast. Nobody can fire this inexpensive replica. Expert gunsmiths, to duplicate an original as closely as possible, handcrafted the other type of replica. This type of replica was very expensive. Most of them cost over $5,000.00, and I found one specimen for which the gunsmith was asking $12,000.00. Considering current labor rates and service charges, and having spent several years of my life as a precision instrument mechanic and toolmaker, I was not surprised. I asked myself, why would anyone pay a high price for a replica when less costly originals were available? In addition, why would anyone want to spend even more money to make the replica look older by pitting its steel barrel and lock-plate? If my pistol is indeed a replica of the second type, i.e., a gun made of similar material, closely matching the original, and one that can be fired, then I am very fortunate to have obtained it at such a low price. However, I fully believe to this day that my pistol is unquestionably an original firearm. It is just too bad that Paul did not recognize this. His belief that the pistol was a cheap replica robbed him of a valuable addition to his collection.

Paul Black

♣

A month after Paul's death, I received a cursory thank-you card from Joyce. A family member on behalf of her must have sent this card, because two days later I received another card from Joyce, completely hand-written:

"Dear Art and Renate, I want to thank you Art, for your love, caring and generosity to us, for making such a wonderful effort to honour Paul and support us in our terrible times. You have no idea how much I appreciate what you did, by making such a warm hearted, long journey, to be with us at his funeral. Paul treasured your friendship over the years, and I appreciate your generous effort – it did lift my spirits (I can't believe you came all that way, so quickly) and I know Paul would also be thankful. He suffered terribly the last 10 days – none of us dreamed he would die, and so we are all in shock even now. Please pray for us, I know Paul is happy, and at peace (with Raymund) but it's a struggle to live without him – he was so wonderful. Renate – take care of Art; he's a treasure. Love, Joyce and family."

Well, please believe me, this special card really made my day. I wasted no time to reply to Joyce. I thanked her for her kind card and told her that I've been thinking of Paul a lot in the past four weeks. I was thinking of all the good times we've had together, and that, even though he's left us temporarily, we have all the memories with him for whom we can be thankful. I told her as well that when I think of Paul I also think of my poem: *I'll Journey On...*[8]

Two weeks later, I gave Joyce a phone call to find out how she's coming along. She said she has her ups and downs. "I still can't believe that Paul died of ALS.[9] Just before he died, he called my name several times, loud and clear, no slurred speech at all. More likely," she said, "he starved to death. If you ever come across something, in your reading, or on the internet, that stimulates the appetite, Art, please let me know about it." Well, who knows? The symptoms of ALS may vary at times, so that a return of clear speech may raise new hope. Any after-the-fact speculations can only cause needless aggravations.

Even though Paul and I had a demanding and strict business relationship, I always considered him one of my closer friends. I shall sincerely miss him, and I will always cherish my memories of the good times we have had together.

---

[8] I'll journey on/my task is done! I've traveled well/through heaven's hell. To stand this trial/was worth my while: I've learned to live/and love and give. I do not leave/to cause you grief –/I have to go/and help you so! But in my heart/I'll only part/to join with thee/for eternity. Now do not cry/and ask not "Why?" Go seek and find/to which we're blind!

[9] ALS stands for amyotrophic lateral sclerosis, better known as Lou Gehrig's disease.

Appendix:

Strange Assertions

This book would not be complete without a few quotations from characters that have given food for thought in my life. I have added my comment to each assertion *(in italics)* to let the reader know my thoughts on it. No doubt, each reader will have his or her own thoughts regarding the intended meaning. So be it.

∞

...we human beings are not responsible to each other. We cannot really give each other anything, not even love. And we cannot really take anything away from each other, not even life.

This assertion by Robert van Gulik, in his book The Given Day, *is strange indeed. Mr. van Gulik was well versed in Chinese literature, and the assertion may come from this area. In any case, if we ponder over it long enough, we may get some special insight into life's mysteries.*

∞

Put forth to watch, unschooled, alone,
'Twixt hostile earth and sky–
The mottled lizard 'neath the stone
Is wiser here than I.

Rudyard Kipling makes an interesting comparison between human beings and animals: Eons of human development and accumulation of wisdom have not yet raised us above the mottled lizard.

Arthur O.R. Thormann

♣

Many waters cannot quench love, neither can floods drown it: If a man would give all the substance of his house for love, it would utterly be contemned.

This quote from the Song of Solomon (8:7) *simply tells us that we cannot buy love.*

∞

If life has any value, it is this that it has none.

Strange, how Karen Blixen, aka Karen Isak, arrived at this conclusion. Was this part of the religion she followed, or was it because of an unfortunate experience she has had?

∞

If time lacks, there is always eternity.

This is a typical Henry Miller assertion. He is clearly mocking the haste that often governs our lives.

∞

Nobody running at full speed has either a head or a heart.

W.B. Yeats takes our haste one step farther: to mindlessness and heartlessness.

∞

The object of war is not to die for your country but to make the other bastard die for his.

This is an interesting assertion by General George Patton. No doubt, both sides have taken it earnestly to heart.

Strange Assertions

Doing a thing well is often a waste of time.

Robert Byrne tells us that a useless task stays useless, even if it is well done.

∞

In the end, everything is a gag.

This assertion by Charlie Chaplin is worthwhile to keep in mind. I have personally experienced it once, after a period of harrowing employment.

∞

You have a thousand friends,
and when you need one, you can't find him;
but one enemy will follow you everywhere you go!

I do not know where I have picked up this quote, but it should serve to warn us against making enemies.

∞

If man has any greatness in him, it comes to light,
not in one flamboyant hour,
but in the ledger of his daily work.

In other words, Beryl Markham asserts that our daily activity as opposed to idleness will bring out our potential greatness.

∞

Everybody's somebody's fool.

Thanks, Orson Wells! So, I guess, we are all fools.

∞

♣

You can live a lifetime, and, at the end of it,
know more about other people than you know about
yourself.

*This assertion by Beryl Markham tells us that we do not often look at
ourselves hard enough.*

∞

The path is the same, for god and for man,
the same for the vegetable as for the star.

*Here, Henry Miller tells us that even God cannot escape His laws.
This assertion should give those who seek God's favours something to
ponder.*

∞

The difference between a career and a job is that a job
gets you nowhere. If you plan a career, then a job
should be a step toward a definite goal–when you
accept a job, you should know exactly when you
intend to leave it.

*Here, Shirley Conran tells us that a job should only be a means to an
end.*

∞

Men cannot change their natures.
All they can do is change their situations.

*This belief by David Hume is worthwhile to keep in mind whenever we
feel like changing our fellow human beings.*

∞

Strange Assertions

♣

Only the mediocre are always at their best.

This assertion by Jean Giraudoux also means that the mediocre are not likely to get any better.

∞

If you have something to say, say it beautifully.

My friend Ed Zacharko was also an accomplished painter; that is probably what explains his assertion.

∞

You don't have to be smart, as long as you're lucky.

This assertion by Barbara Frum was also shared by Napoleon Bonaparte, when he picked generals for his battles.

∞

There's no life except by death; there is no vision but by faith.

This simple assertion by Nitti, The Enforcer *(see the movie) is all too often overlooked by us.*

∞

The Americans are our best friends, whether we like it or not.

Robert Thompson probably wanted to tell us not to kick Big Brother too hard.

∞

129

Arthur O.R. Thormann

♣

He who is not busy being born is busy dying.

Here, Bob Dylan's message is: Recreate yourself constantly; otherwise, you will surely deteriorate.

∞

I've learned not to believe in magical leaders anymore; character and compassion are more important than ideology; even if it's absurd to think you can try to change things, it's even more absurd to think that it's foolish and unimportant to try.

In other words, Peter C. Newman tells us not to give up trying to change things.

∞

The minute you establish an organization, it starts to decay.

I agree with Tony Paskett. In fact, this assertion also applies to modern computers.

∞

Everything is designed that way.

This is my Grandmother Henriette Jeske's simple explanation for the world's mysteries.

∞

What people think is far more important than the facts.

Nobody who has ever been involved in negotiations will disagree with Arnold Hartpence.

Strange Assertions

♣

We're born alone, we live alone, and we die alone;
as long as we realize this and come to accept it,
we'll appreciate more the few times when we're not
alone.

*This contradiction by Yul Brynner tells us more about him than about
ourselves.*

∞

You can get anything you want, but you have to do
more than ask.

This assertion by Roger Dawson applies only sometimes.

∞

The world is what it is; men who are nothing,
who allow themselves to become nothing, have no
place in it.

This strange assertion by V.S. Naipaul in his book A Bend in the River
will surely stimulate your questioning mind.

∞

Genuine love comes from God within you.

*This is my only assertion included in this list. I have arrived at it by a
simple deduction: Jesus told us to love our enemies; this takes a
superhuman effort; therefore, if such superhuman love actually exists
in any one of us, it must surely come from God.*
Amen.

∞

Arthur O.R. Thormann

♣

About the Author

Arthur and his wife, Renate, reside in Edmonton, the capital of sunny Alberta, a province of Canada.